COSMETOLOGY
CERTIFICATION EXAM

COSMETOLOGY
CERTIFICATION EXAM

4th Edition

NEW YORK

Published in the United States by LearningExpress, LLC, New York.

Library of Congress Cataloging-in-Publication Data
Cosmetology certification exam—4th ed.
p. cm.
ISBN-13: 978-1-57685-698-7 (pbk. : alk. paper)
ISBN-10: 1-57685-698-4 (pbk. : alk. paper)
1. Beauty culture—United States—Examinations, questions, etc. 2. Beauty operators—Licenses—United States—Examinations, questions, etc. I. LearningExpress (Organization)
TT958.C66 2009
646.7'2076—dc22

2009016504

Printed in the United States of America

9 8 7 6 5 4 3 2 1

Fourth Edition

ISBN 978-1-57685-698-7

For information on LearningExpress, other LearningExpress products,
or bulk sales, please write to us at:
LearningExpress
2 Rector Street
26th Floor
New York, NY 10006

Or visit us at:
www.learnatest.com

Contents

COSMETOLOGY
CERTIFICATION EXAM

LESSON 1

THE COSMETOLOGY EXAM

LESSON SUMMARY

This lesson advises you on how to prepare to take the Cosmetology Exam. It outlines the contents of the exam and gives you some tips about how to use this book to study for it.

Each state's board of cosmetology sets certification standards for cosmetologists, manicurists, and estheticians. Although requirements and certification proceedings differ somewhat by state, most require both a written exam and a practical exam, and all are based on the same core content you studied in your cosmetology course.

Three main companies provide cosmetology written tests throughout the United States. These companies are PSI (Psychological Services, Inc.), Thomson Prometric, and NIC (National Interstate Council of State Boards of Cosmetology, Inc.).

Thirty-two states (including Guam and Washington, D.C.) use exams sponsored by NIC. Another 12 states use exams sponsored by Thomson Prometric. PSI handles only the state of Tennessee. All three testing companies create exams for state boards of cosmetology that encourage high standards for entry into the profession. Whether your state uses Thomson Prometric, an NIC, or a PSI exam, you will be tested on the fundamentals that you learned in your cosmetology course.

A list of specific certification requirements for all 50 states, as well as contact information for the state boards of cosmetology, can be found starting on page 137 of this book.

For more information about NIC, Thomson Prometric, or PSI, visit their websites, which contain helpful information about the organizations, the tests they develop, and the states they serve.

NATIONAL INTERSTATE COUNCIL OF STATE BOARDS OF COSMETOLOGY, INC. (NIC)
P.O. Box 11390
Columbia, South Carolina 29211
www.nictesting.org

THOMSON PROMETRIC
3110 Lord Baltimore Drive
Suite 200
Baltimore, Maryland 21244
www.prometric.com

PSI EXAMINATION SERVICE
3210 East Tropicana Avenue
Las Vegas, Nevada 89121
1-800-733-9267

The Cosmetology Written Exam

The 100 questions on the Cosmetology Exam are divided into a number of content areas that match the content areas you studied in your cosmetology course. Passing the test means that you have the knowledge required of an entry-level cosmetologist.

Most written examinations for cosmetologists contain questions in four general areas:

- Scientific Concepts
- Hair Care and Services
- Skin Care and Services
- Nail Care and Services

The questions included in the four practice written exams in this book are found in Lessons 3, 5, 6, and 7 and are grouped into these same general categories. The additional practice questions that constitute the Cosmetology Refresher Course in Lesson 4 follow the same format. Keep in mind, however, that while the basic content on each exam will be similar, the category groupings can vary from state to state.

The following table shows the content of each practice exam in this book, broken down in a system that is similar to that used for most state exams. The table also lists the subtopics included under each main topic and the number of questions the exams typically contain for those topics. The subtopics will reflect the topics you studied in your cosmetology course and the chapters in your textbook.

Because not all states use the same exam, the exams in this book contain questions that cover all the possible topic areas, such as the business of running a beauty salon, presenting yourself as a professional, and the basics of massage and hair removal. Therefore, no matter what state you live in or what specific content is covered on the exam you take, this book will help you prepare for your exam.

Scientific Concepts: 30%

Infection Control

- Microbiology
- Methods of infection control
- Federal regulations and universal precautions

Human Anatomy and Physiology

- Cells
- Tissues
- Body systems

Nutrition

Ergonomics

Basic Principles of Chemistry

- Compounds, mixtures, solutions, suspensions, and emulsions
- The pH scale
- Product ingredients
- Chemical reactions

Basic Principles of Electricity

- Electric current
- Electric measurements
- Electricity in cosmetology
- Safety precautions and infection control

Hair Care and Services: 50%

Trichology

- Properties and structure of hair and scalp
- Hair analysis and hair quality
- Hair growth
- Hair loss (alopecia)
- Disorders of the scalp

Principles of Hair Design

- Elements of hair design
- Principles of hair design
- Facial shapes

Draping Procedures

- Wet services
- Dry services
- Chemical services

Brushing, Shampooing, Conditioning, and Hair and Scalp Treatment Procedures

- Brushing the hair
- Shampooing
- Conditioning
- Hair and scalp treatments
- Safety precautions and infection control

Haircutting Procedures

- Basic principles of haircutting
- Client consultation
- Tools
- Basic haircuts
- Safety precautions and infection control

Hairstyling Procedures

- Client consultation
- Wet styling
- Long hair styling
- Thermal styling
- Safety precautions and infection control

Braiding, Wigs, and Hair Enhancements/Additions

- Client consultation
- Braiding
- Hair extensions/additions
- Wigs
- Hairpieces
- Safety precautions and infection control

Chemical Texture Services

- Client consultation
- Permanent waving
- Chemical hair relaxers
- Soft curl permanent or curl reforming
- Safety precautions and infection control

Hair Coloring Procedures

- Color theory
- Client consultation
- Types of hair color
- Color selection
- Hair color applications
- Hair lightening
- Special effects hair coloring
- Hair color problems and corrections
- Safety precautions and infection control

Skin Care and Services: 10%

Skin Histology

- Anatomy of skin
- Disorders of the skin
- Functions of the skin

Draping Procedures

Hair Removal Procedures
- Client consultation
- Temporary hair removal
- Safety precautions and infection control

Facial Procedures
- Client consultation
- Skin care tools and work area
- Facial massage
- Facial treatments
- Safety precautions and infection control

Facial Makeup Application
- Client consultation
- Cosmetics for facial makeup
- Makeup color theory
- Corrective theory
- Safety precautions and infection control

Nail Care and Services: 10%

Nail Structure and Growth
- Nail growth
- Nail disorders/diseases

Manicure and Pedicure Procedures
- Client consultation
- Nail care tools and work area
- Types of hand and foot massages
- Types of manicures
- Types of pedicures
- Safety precautions and infection control

Advanced Nail Procedures
- Preservice and postservice
- Artificial nail services
- Safety precautions and infection control

The Practical Exam

Virtually every state board of cosmetology requires a practical exam in addition to the written exam. The content included on the exam varies by state, so you must consult your state board for the specific material that will be included on your exam, as well as exactly how that material will be tested.

Regardless of how your state conducts the practical exam, some content areas are considered essential, either to maintain reciprocity of certification from state to state or to meet common job descriptions.

Content areas for the cosmetology practical exam usually include the following key topics:

- Hair Shaping
- Chemical Waving
- Hair Lightening/Hair Coloring
- Chemical Relaxing
- Shaping and Pin Curl Placement
- Thermal Curling
- Blow-Dry Styling

In addition, most states require a number of additions to these subject areas, such as Roller Placement, Facials, Manicuring, and Sculptured Nails.

For each content area in which you are required to demonstrate your competence, you will be given a specific task, all the needed materials, and a time limit. You will be evaluated on your use of proper safety precautions, infection control procedures, and client protection procedures. For example, to demonstrate your competence in chemical waving, you might be directed to wrap the center back section of a head and to section the hair for correct rod placement. You would also be required to demonstrate how to do a test curl. Similar strict guidelines and performance criteria would be given to you for each content area in which you were tested.

Using This Book to Prepare for the Written Test

This book contains 250 review questions in the Cosmetology Refresher Course (Lesson 4), arranged by content grouping, as well as four complete cosmetology practice exams, each containing 100 multiple-choice questions. The practice exam questions are also grouped by content area, since this is the way many state exams are arranged.

The first step in using this book to prepare for your Cosmetology Exam is to read Lesson 2, which presents the nine-step LearningExpress Test Preparation System. This chapter shows you essential test-taking strategies that you can practice as you take the exams in this book.

Your next step is to take the first cosmetology practice exam, Lesson 3, as a pretest. Score your answers using the answer key that follows the exam. Complete explanations for the answers are included in the key.

Remember, the passing score on most exams is approximately 75%. If you score higher than 75% on your first practice test, congratulations! Don't assume that this means you will easily pass the actual test without practice. The test questions on the day of your exam may be different from those on the practice test. Although you are well on your way to passing, you will still need some test preparation. No matter what your initial score is, follow the suggestions in the next paragraphs.

If you score lower than 75% on Cosmetology Practice Exam 1, don't panic. Do put in some concentrated study time, however. Begin by determining your major areas of weakness. For example, suppose you answered 35 of the pretest questions incorrectly, giving you a score of 65, or 65% correct. On rereading the questions you missed, you find that they break down into the following content areas:

- Scientific Concepts: you missed 18 out of 36 answers
- Hair Care and Services: you missed 3 out of 23
- Skin Care and Services: you missed 10 out of 20
- Nail Care and Services: you missed 3 out of 21

In this example, your analysis tells you that you need to devote extra study time to two areas: Scientific Concepts and Skin Care and Services. Try putting in one or two evenings of study specifically on each of these areas. First, check the content breakdown on pages 2–4 to make sure you understand what topics are included in each area. Then, review all materials on these topics in your cosmetology textbook and printed materials.

Now that you have taken and analyzed the pretest and reviewed some weak areas, it is time to use Lesson 4, the Cosmetology Refresher Course. Don't treat this 250-question review as a test, even though the questions have been purposely set in the same multiple-choice format of an actual exam.

One strategy for using the Cosmetology Refresher Course is to answer all the questions within one content area (each has a heading) and then review all the answer explanations in that section. Move on to the next section and do the same. This process should reinforce correct answers and immediately modify wrong answers.

Another idea is to take the questions from your weakest content area and copy them onto flash cards. Take the flash cards with you wherever you go. If you have some downtime—say, waiting for an appointment or in line at the grocery store—you can test yourself with your flash cards.

After you have spent some time on the Cosmetology Refresher Course, you should feel ready to take Practice Exam 2 in Lesson 5. Once again, check your total score and content area breakdown. Chances are that both will have improved.

In the time leading up to the Cosmetology Exam, use the two remaining exams (Lessons 6 and 7) to further pinpoint areas of weakness to review. For example, you may find that now you do very well on all Hair Care and Services questions except those that concern hair relaxing. That knowledge tells you what specific materials to review.

Once you have worked on and improved your areas of weakness, use the final days before the test to keep fresh and do some general brushing-up on your knowledge and your test-taking skills. Devote a short period of time each day to reviewing several chapters of your textbook. Use the third and fourth practice exams to rehearse test-taking strategies and procedures.

After reading and studying this book, you'll be well on your way to passing the Cosmetology Exam. Good luck as you advance in this rewarding and glamorous career!

LESSON

THE LEARNINGEXPRESS TEST PREPARATION SYSTEM

LESSON SUMMARY

Taking the Cosmetology Exam can be tough. It demands a lot of preparation if you want to achieve a top score. Your career depends on your passing the exam. The LearningExpress Test Preparation System, developed exclusively for LearningExpress by leading test experts, gives you the discipline and attitude you need to be a winner.

First, the bad news: Taking the Cosmetology Exam is no picnic, and neither is getting ready for it. Your future career as a cosmetologist depends on your getting a passing score, but there are all sorts of pitfalls that can keep you from doing your best on this all-important exam. Here are some of the obstacles that can stand in the way of your success:

- Being unfamiliar with the format of the exam
- Being paralyzed by test anxiety
- Leaving your preparation to the last minute
- Not preparing at all!
- Not knowing vital test-taking skills: how to pace yourself through the exam, how to use the process of elimination, and when to guess
- Not being in tip-top mental and physical shape
- Arriving late at the test site, having to work on an empty stomach, or shivering through the exam because the room is cold

What's the common denominator in all these test-taking pitfalls? One word: control. Who's in control, you or the exam?

Now the good news: The LearningExpress Test Preparation System puts you in control. In just nine easy-to-follow steps, you will learn everything you need to know to make sure that you are in charge of your preparation for and your performance on the exam. Other test takers may let the test get the better of them; other test takers may be unprepared or out of shape, but not you. You will have taken all the steps you need to take to get a high score on the Cosmetology Exam.

Here's how the LearningExpress Test Preparation System works: Nine easy steps lead you through everything you need to know and do to get ready to master your exam. Each of the steps listed here includes both reading about the step and one or more activities. It's important that you do the activities along with the reading, or you won't be getting the full benefit of the system. Each step tells you approximately how much time that step will take you to complete.

Step 1. Get Information	50 minutes
Step 2. Conquer Test Anxiety	20 minutes
Step 3. Make a Plan	30 minutes
Step 4. Learn to Manage Your Time	10 minutes
Step 5. Learn to Use the Process of Elimination	20 minutes
Step 6. Know When to Guess	20 minutes
Step 7. Reach Your Peak Performance Zone	10 minutes
Step 8. Get Your Act Together	10 minutes
Step 9. Do It!	10 minutes
Total	**3 hours**

We estimate that working through the entire system will take you approximately three hours, although it's perfectly okay if you work faster or slower than the time estimates assume. If you can take an afternoon or evening, you can work through the whole LearningExpress Test Preparation System in one sitting. Otherwise, you can break it up and do just one or two steps a day for the next several days. It's up to you—remember, you're in control.

Step 1: Get Information

Time to complete: 50 minutes
Activities: Read Lesson 1, "The Cosmetology Exam," and Lesson 9, "Certification Requirements"
Knowledge is power. The first step in the LearningExpress Test Preparation System is finding out everything you can about the Cosmetology Exam. Once you have your information, the next steps in the LearningExpress Test Preparation System will show you what to do about it.

Part A: Straight Talk about the Cosmetology Exam

The cosmetology written exam is just one part of a whole series of evaluations you have to go through to show that you are prepared to perform the many, varied tasks of a cosmetologist. The written exam attempts to measure your knowledge of your trade. The practical skills exam attempts to measure your ability to apply what you know.

It's important for you to remember that your score on the cosmetology written exam does not determine how smart you are or even whether you will make a good cosmetologist. There are all kinds of things a written exam like this can't test: whether you are likely to show up late or call in sick a lot, whether you have the interpersonal skills necessary to build the trusting, comfortable relationships that will keep your clients coming back, and whether you have an enthusiastic dedication to learning and performing your trade well. Those kinds of things are hard to evaluate, while your ability to fill in the right little circles on a bubble answer sheet is easy to evaluate.

This is not to say that filling in the right little circles is not important! The knowledge tested on the written exam is knowledge you will need to do your job. And your ability to enter the profession you've trained for depends on passing this exam. And that's why you're here—using the LearningExpress Test Preparation System to achieve control over the exam.

Part B: What's on the Test

If you haven't already done so, stop here and read Lesson 1 of this book, which gives you an overview of the typical cosmetology written exams.

Always keep in mind that states use different exams. Turn to Lesson 9 for a state-by-state boards overview. If you haven't already gotten the full rundown on certification procedures as part of your train ing program, you can contact your state cosmetology agency listed in Lesson 9 for details.

Step 2: Conquer Test Anxiety

Time to complete: 20 minutes
Activity: Take the Test Stress Test

Having complete information about the exam is the first step in getting control of the exam. Next, you have to overcome one of the biggest obstacles to test success: test anxiety. Test anxiety not only impairs your performance on the exam itself, but can also even keep you from preparing! In Step 2, you will learn stress management techniques that will help you succeed on your exam. Learn these strategies now, and practice them as you work through the exams in this book, so they'll be second nature to you by exam day.

Combatting Test Anxiety

The first thing you need to know is that a little test anxiety is a good thing. Everyone gets nervous before a big exam—and if that nervousness motivates you to prepare thoroughly, so much the better. It's said that Sir Laurence Olivier, one of the foremost British actors of this century, threw up before every performance. His stage fright didn't impair his performance; in fact, it probably gave him a little extra edge—just the kind of edge you need to do well, whether on a stage or in an examination room.

Following is the Test Stress Test. Stop here and answer these questions to find out whether your level of test anxiety is something you should worry about.

Stress Management before the Test

If you feel your level of anxiety getting the best of you in the weeks before the test, here is what you need to do to bring the level down again:

- **Get prepared.** There's nothing like knowing what to expect and being prepared for it to put you in control of test anxiety. That's why you're reading this book. Use it faithfully, and remind yourself that you're better prepared than most of the people taking the test.
- **Practice self-confidence.** A positive attitude is a great way to combat test anxiety. This is no time to be humble or shy. Stand in front of the mirror and say to your reflection, "I'm prepared. I'm full of self-confidence. I'm going to ace this test. I know I can do it." Say it into a tape recorder and play it back once a day. If you hear it often enough, you will believe it.
- **Fight negative messages.** Every time someone starts telling you how hard the exam is or how it's almost impossible to get a high score, start telling them your self-confidence messages. If the someone with the negative messages is you telling yourself you don't do well on exams and you just can't do this, don't listen. Turn on your tape recorder and listen to your self-confidence messages.
- **Visualize.** Imagine yourself reporting for duty on your first day as a cosmetologist. Think of yourself at a fashion shoot, styling the hair and making up the faces of top models—you're part of the action. Visualizing success can help make it happen—and

Test Stress Test

You need to worry about test anxiety only if it is extreme enough to impair your performance. The following questionnaire will provide a diagnosis of your level of test anxiety. In the blank before each statement, write the number that most accurately describes your experience.

0 = Never

1 = Once or twice

2 = Sometimes

3 = Often

___I have gotten so nervous before an exam that I simply put down the books and didn't study for it.

___I have experienced disabling physical symptoms such as vomiting and severe headaches because I was nervous about an exam.

___I have simply not showed up for an exam because I was scared to take it.

___I have experienced dizziness and disorientation while taking an exam.

___I have had trouble filling in the little circles because my hands were shaking too hard.

___I have failed an exam because I was too nervous to complete it.

___**Total: Add up the numbers in the blanks above.**

Your Test Stress Score

Here are the steps you should take, depending on your score. If you scored:

- **Below 3**, your level of test anxiety is nothing to worry about; it's probably just enough to give you that little extra edge.
- **Between 3 and 6**, your test anxiety may be enough to impair your performance, and you should practice the stress management techniques listed in this section to try to bring your test anxiety down to manageable levels.
- **Above 6**, your level of test anxiety is a serious concern. In addition to practicing the stress management techniques listed in this section, you may want to seek additional, personal help. Call your local high school or community college and ask for the academic counselor. Tell the counselor that you have a level of test anxiety that sometimes keeps you from being able to take the exam. The counselor may be willing to help you or may suggest someone else you should talk to.

it reminds you of why you're going through all this work in preparing for the exam.

- **Exercise.** Physical activity helps calm your body down and focus your mind. Besides, being in good physical shape can actually help you do well on the exam. Go for a run, lift weights, go swimming—and do it regularly.

Stress Management on Test Day

There are several ways you can bring down your level of test anxiety on test day. These methods work best if you practice them in the weeks before the test, so you know which ones work for you.

- **Deep breathing.** Take a deep breath while you count to five. Hold it for a count of one, and then let it out on a count of five. Repeat several times.
- **Move your body.** Try rolling your head in a circle. Rotate your shoulders. Shake your hands from the wrist. Many people find these movements very relaxing.
- **Visualize again.** Think of the place where you are most relaxed: lying on the beach in the sun, walking through the park, or whatever. Now close your eyes and imagine you're actually there. If you practice in advance, you'll find that you need only a few seconds of this exercise to experience a significant increase in your sense of well-being.

When anxiety threatens to overwhelm you right there during the exam, there are still things you can do to manage the stress level:

- **Repeat your self-confidence messages.** You should have them memorized by now. Say them quietly to yourself, and believe them!
- **Visualize one more time.** This time, visualize yourself moving smoothly and quickly through the test, answering every question right and finishing just before time is up. Like most visualization techniques, this one works best if you've practiced it ahead of time.
- **Find an easy question.** Skim over the test until you find an easy question, and answer it. Getting even one circle filled in gets you into the test-taking groove.
- **Take a mental break.** Everyone loses concentration once in a while during a long test. It's normal, so you shouldn't worry about it. Instead, accept what has happened. Say to yourself, "Hey, I lost it there for a minute. My brain is taking a break." Put down your pencil, close your eyes, and do some deep breathing for a few seconds. Then you're ready to go back to work.

Try these techniques ahead of time, and see if they work for you!

Step 3: Make a Plan

Time to complete: 30 minutes
Activity: Construct a study plan

Maybe the most important thing you can do to get control of yourself and your exam is to make a study plan. Too many people fail to prepare simply because they fail to plan. Spending hours on the day before the exam poring over sample test questions not only raises your level of test anxiety, but also is simply no substitute for careful preparation and practice over time.

Don't fall into the cram trap. Take control of your preparation time by mapping out a study schedule. On the following pages are two sample schedules, based on the amount of time you have before you take the cosmetology written exam. If you're the kind of person who needs deadlines and assignments to motivate you for a project, here they are. If you're the kind of person who doesn't like to follow other people's plans, you can use the suggested schedules here to construct your own.

Even more important than making a plan is making a commitment. You can't review everything you learned in your cosmetology course in one night.

You have to set aside some time every day for study and practice. Try for at least 20 minutes a day. Twenty minutes daily will do you much more good than two hours on Saturday.

Don't put off your study until the day before the exam. Start now. A few minutes a day, with half an hour or more on weekends, can make a big difference in your score.

Schedule A: The 30-Day Plan

If you have at least a month before you take the Cosmetology Exam, you have plenty of time to prepare—as long as you don't waste it! If you have less than a month, turn to Schedule B.

TIME	PREPARATION
Days 1–4	Skim over the written materials from your training program, particularly noting 1) areas you expect to be emphasized on the exam and 2) areas you don't remember well. On Day 4, concentrate on those areas.
Day 5	Take the first practice exam found in Lesson 3.
Day 6	Score the first practice exam. Use the outline of skills on the test given in Lesson 1 to show you which are your strongest and weakest areas. Identify two areas that you will concentrate on before you take the second practice exam.
Days 7–10	Study the two areas you identified as your weak points. Use the Refresher Course in Lesson 4 for extra practice in these areas.
Day 11	Take the second practice exam in Lesson 5.
Day 12	Score the second practice exam. Identify one area to concentrate on before you take the third practice exam.
Days 13–18	Study the one area you identified for review. Again, use the Refresher Course in Lesson 4 for extra practice in this area.
Day 19	Take the third practice exam found in Lesson 6.
Day 20	Once again, identify one area to review, based on your score on the third practice exam.
Days 20–21	Study the one area you identified for review, using the Refresher Course in Lesson 4 for extra practice.
Days 22–25	Take an overview of all your training materials, consolidating your strengths and improving on your weaknesses.
Days 26–27	Review all the areas that have given you the most trouble in the three practice exams you've taken so far.
Day 28	Take the fourth practice exam in Lesson 7. Note how much you've improved!
Day 29	Review one or two weak areas, doing any sample questions in these areas from Lesson 4 that you haven't already done.
Day before the exam	Relax. Do something unrelated to the exam and go to bed at a reasonable hour.

Schedule B: The Ten-Day Plan

If you have two weeks or less before you take the exam, you may have your work cut out for you. Use this ten-day schedule to help you make the most of your time.

TIME	PREPARATION
Day 1	Take the first practice exam in Lesson 3 and score it using the answer key at the end. Turn to the list of subject areas on the exam in Lesson 1, and find out which areas need the most work, based on your exam score.
Day 2	Review one area that gave you trouble on the first practice exam. Use the Refresher Course in Lesson 4 for extra practice in these areas.
Day 3	Review another area that gave you trouble on the first practice exam. Again, use the questions in Lesson 4 for extra practice.
Day 4	Take the second practice exam in Lesson 5 and score it.
Day 5	If your score on the second practice exam doesn't show improvement on the two areas you studied, review them. If you did improve in those areas, choose a new weak area to study today.
Day 6	Take the third practice exam in Lesson 6 and score it.
Day 7	Choose your weakest area from the third practice exam to review. Use the Refresher Course in Lesson 4 for extra practice.
Day 8	Review any areas that you have not yet covered in this schedule.
Day 9	Take the fourth practice exam in Lesson 7 and score it.
Day 10	Use your last study day to brush up on any areas that are still giving you trouble. Do any sample questions in those areas from Lesson 4 that you haven't already done.
Day before the exam	Relax. Do something unrelated to the exam and go to bed at a reasonable hour.

Step 4: Learn to Manage Your Time

Time to complete: 10 minutes to read, many hours of practice!
Activities: Practice these strategies as you take the sample tests in this book

Steps 4, 5, and 6 of the LearningExpress Test Preparation System put you in charge of your exam by showing you test-taking strategies that work. Practice these strategies as you take the sample tests in this book, and then you'll be ready to use them on test day.

First, you will take control of your time on the exam. Most cosmetology exams have a time limit, which may give you more than enough time to complete all the questions—or may not. It's a terrible feeling to hear the examiner say, "Five minutes left," when you're only three-quarters of the way through the test. Here are some tips to keep that from happening to you.

- **Follow directions.** If the directions are given orally, listen to them. If they're written on the exam booklet, read them carefully. Ask questions before the exam begins if there's anything you don't understand. If you're allowed to write in your exam booklet, write down the beginning time and the ending time of the exam.
- **Pace yourself.** Glance at your watch every few minutes, and compare the time to how far you've gotten in the test. When one-quarter of the time has elapsed, you should be one-quarter of the way through the test, and so on. If you're falling behind, pick up the pace a bit.
- **Keep moving.** Don't dither around on one question. If you don't know the answer, skip the question and move on. Circle the number of the question in your test booklet in case you have time to come back to it later.
- **Keep track of your place on the answer sheet.** If you skip a question, make sure you skip it on the answer sheet, too. Check yourself every five to ten questions to make sure the question number and the answer sheet number are still the same.
- **Don't rush.** Although you should keep moving, rushing won't help. Try to keep calm and work methodically and quickly.

Step 5: Learn to Use the Process of Elimination

Time to complete: 20 minutes
Activity: Complete Using the Process of Elimination worksheet

After time management, your next most important tool for taking control of your exam is using the process of elimination wisely. It's standard test-taking wisdom that you should always read all the answer choices before choosing your answer. This helps you find the right answer by eliminating wrong answer choices. And, sure enough, that standard wisdom applies to your exam, too.

Let's say you're facing a question that goes like this:

12. Trichology is the study of
a. hair.
b. beauty.
c. magic.
d. cards.

You should always use the process of elimination on a question like this, even if the right answer jumps out at you. Sometimes, the answer that jumps out isn't right after all. Let's assume, for the purpose of this exercise, that you're a little rusty on your terminology, so you need to use a little intuition to make up for what you don't remember. Proceed through the answer choices in order.

So, you start with choice **a.** "Hair" looks like a good choice; after all, a good deal of what you study has to do with hair, and the word *trichology* sounds very familiar to you. Put a check mark next to choice **a**, meaning "good answer, I might use this one."

On to the next. "Beauty" looks good, since beauty is another subject you've studied in depth. But you know that words associated with beauty usually begin with *belle* or *beau*. Put a question mark next to choice **b**, meaning "well, maybe."

Choice **c** doesn't seem likely. Why would the test makers ask you a question about magic? Put an **X** next to this one so you never have to look at it again.

Choice **d** seems just as unlikely. What do cards have to do with being a cosmetologist? It's safe to put an **X** next to this one, too.

Now your question looks like this:

12. Trichology is the study of
✓ **a.** hair.
? **b.** beauty.
X **c.** magic.
X **d.** cards.

You've got just one check mark, for a good answer. If you're pressed for time, you should simply mark choice **a** on your answer sheet. If you've got the time to be extra careful, you could compare your check-mark answer to your question-mark answers to make sure that it's better.

It's good to have a system for marking good, bad, and maybe answers. We recommend this one:

X = bad
✓ = good
? = maybe

If you don't like these marks, devise your own system. Just make sure you do it long before test day—while you're working through the practice exams in this book—so you won't have to worry about it during the test.

Even when you think you're absolutely clueless about a question, you can often use process of elimination to get rid of one answer choice. If so, you're better prepared to make an educated guess, as you'll see in Step 6. More often, the process of elimination allows you to get down to only two possibly right answers. Then you're in a strong position to guess. And sometimes, even though you don't know the right answer, you find it simply by getting rid of the wrong ones, as you did in the previous example.

Try using your powers of elimination on the questions in the Using the Process of Elimination worksheet that follows. The questions aren't about cosmetology work; they're just designed to show you how the process of elimination works. The answer explanations for this worksheet show one possible way you might use the process to arrive at the right answer.

The process of elimination is your tool for the next step, which is knowing when to guess.

Step 6: Know When to Guess

Time to complete: 20 minutes
Activity: Complete the Your Guessing Ability worksheet

Armed with the process of elimination, you're ready to take control of one of the big questions in test taking: Should I guess? The first and main answer is yes. Some exams have what's called a "guessing penalty," in which a fraction of your wrong answers is subtracted from your right answers—but cosmetology exams don't tend to work like that. The number of questions you answer correctly yields your raw score. So, you have nothing to lose and everything to gain by guessing.

The more complicated answer to the question "Should I guess?" depends on you—your personality and your "guessing intuition." There are two things you need to know about yourself before you go into the exam:

Using the Process of Elimination

Use the process of elimination to answer the following questions.

1. Ilsa is as old as Meghan will be in five years. The difference between Ed's age and Meghan's age is twice the difference between Ilsa's age and Meghan's age. Ed is 29. How old is Ilsa?
a. 4
b. 10
c. 19
d. 24

2. "All drivers of commercial vehicles must carry a valid commercial driver's license whenever operating a commercial vehicle."
According to this sentence, which of the following people need NOT carry a commercial driver's license?
a. a truck driver idling his engine while waiting to be directed to a loading dock
b. a bus operator backing her bus out of the way of another bus in the bus lot
c. a taxi driver driving his personal car to the grocery store
d. a limousine driver taking the limousine to her home after dropping off her last passenger of the evening

3. Smoking tobacco has been linked to
a. increased risk of stroke and heart attack.
b. all forms of respiratory disease.
c. increasing mortality rates over the past ten years.
d. juvenile delinquency.

4. Which of the following words is spelled correctly?
a. incorrigible
b. outragous
c. domestickated
d. understandible

Answers

Here are the answers, as well as some suggestions as to how you might have used the process of elimination to find them.

1. d. You should have eliminated choice **a** right off the bat. Ilsa can't be four years old if Meghan is going to be Ilsa's age in five years. The best way to eliminate other answer choices is to try plugging them in to the information given in the problem. For instance, for choice **b**, if Ilsa is 10, then Meghan must be 5. The difference between their ages is 5. The difference between Ed's age, 29, and Meghan's age, 5, is 24. Is 24 two times 5? No. Then choice **b** is wrong. You could eliminate choice **c** in the same way and be left with choice **d**.

2. c. Note the word *not* in the question, and go through the answers one by one. Is the truck driver in choice **a** "operating a commercial vehicle"? Yes, idling counts as "operating," so he needs to have a commercial driver's license. Likewise, the bus operator in choice **b** is operating a commercial vehicle; the question doesn't say the operator has to be on the street. The limo driver in choice **d** is operating

Using the Process of Elimination (continued)

a commercial vehicle, even if it doesn't have a passenger in it. However, the cabbie in choice **c** is not operating a commercial vehicle, but his own private car.

3. a. You could eliminate choice **b** simply because of the presence of the word *all*. Such absolutes hardly ever appear in correct answer choices. Choice **c** looks attractive until you think a little about what you know—aren't fewer people smoking these days, rather than more? So how could smoking be responsible for a higher mortality rate? (If you didn't know that mortality rate means the rate at which people die, you might keep this choice as a possibility, but you would still be able to eliminate two answers and have only two to choose from.) And choice **d** is plain silly, so you could eliminate that one, too. You are left with the correct choice, **a**.

4. a. How you used the process of elimination here depends on which words you recognized as being spelled incorrectly. If you knew that the correct spellings were outrageous, domesticated, and understandable, then you were home free. Surely you knew that at least one of those words was wrong!

Your Guessing Ability

The following are ten really hard questions. You are not supposed to know the answers. Rather, this is an assessment of your ability to guess when you don't have a clue. Read each question carefully, as if you were expected to answer it. If you have any knowledge of the subject, use that knowledge to help you eliminate wrong answer choices.

1. September 7 is Independence Day in
a. India.
b. Costa Rica.
c. Brazil.
d. Australia.

2. Which of the following is the formula for determining the momentum of an object?
a. $p = MV$
b. $F = ma$
c. $P = IV$
d. $E = mc^2$

3. Because of the expansion of the universe, the stars and other celestial bodies are all moving away from each other. This phenomenon is known as
a. Newton's first law.
b. the big bang.
c. gravitational collapse.
d. Hubble flow.

4. American author Gertrude Stein was born in
a. 1713.
b. 1830.
c. 1874.
d. 1901.

5. Which of the following is NOT one of the Five Classics attributed to Confucius?
a. *I Ching*
b. *Book of Holiness*
c. *Spring and Autumn Annals*
d. *Book of History*

6. The religious and philosophical doctrine that holds that the universe is constantly in a struggle between good and evil is known as
a. Pelagianism.
b. Manichaeanism.
c. neo-Hegelianism.
d. Epicureanism.

7. The third Chief Justice of the U.S. Supreme Court was
   a. John Blair.
   b. William Cushing.
   c. James Wilson.
   d. John Jay.

8. Which of the following is the poisonous portion of a daffodil?
   a. the bulb
   b. the leaves
   c. the stem
   d. the flowers

9. The winner of the Masters golf tournament in 1953 was
   a. Sam Snead.
   b. Cary Middlecoff.
   c. Arnold Palmer.
   d. Ben Hogan.

10. The state with the highest per capita personal income in 1980 was
    a. Alaska.
    b. Connecticut.
    c. New York.
    d. Texas.

Answers

Check your answers against the following correct answers.

1. **c.**
2. **a.**
3. **d.**
4. **c.**
5. **b.**
6. **b.**
7. **b.**
8. **a.**
9. **d.**
10. **a.**

How Did You Do?

You may have simply gotten lucky and actually known the answer to one or two questions. In addition, your guessing was probably more successful if you were able to use the process of elimination on any of the questions. Maybe you didn't know who the third Chief Justice was (question 7), but you knew that John Jay was the first. In that case, you would have eliminated choice **d** and, therefore, improved your odds of guessing right from one in four to one in three.

According to probability, you should get two-and-a-half answers correct, so getting either two or three right would be average. If you got four or more right, you may be a really terrific guesser. If you got one or none right, you may be a really bad guesser.

Keep in mind, though, that this is only a small sample. You should continue to keep track of your guessing ability as you work through the sample questions in this book. Circle the numbers of questions you guess on as you make your guess; or, if you don't have time while you take the practice tests, go back afterward and try to remember which questions you guessed on. Remember, on a test with four answer choices, your chance of guessing correctly is one in four. So keep a separate "guessing" score for each exam. How many questions did you guess on? How many did you get right? If the number you got right is at least one-fourth of the number of questions you guessed on, you are at least an average guesser—maybe better—and you should always go ahead and guess on the real exam. If the number you got right is significantly lower than one-fourth of the number you guessed on, you need to improve your guessing skills.

- Are you a risk taker?
- Are you a good guesser?

You will have to decide about your risk-taking quotient on your own. To find out if you're a good guesser, complete the Your Guessing Ability worksheet. Frankly, even if you're a play-it-safe person with lousy intuition, you're still safe in guessing every time. The best thing would be if you could overcome your anxieties and go ahead and mark an answer. But you may want to have a sense of how good your intuition is before you go into the exam.

Step 7: Reach Your Peak Performance Zone

Time to complete: 10 minutes to read; weeks to complete!
Activity: Complete the Physical Preparation Checklist
To get ready for a challenge like a big exam, you have to take control of your physical, as well as your mental, state. Exercise, proper diet, and rest will ensure that your body works with, rather than against, your mind on test day, as well as during your preparation.

Exercise

If you don't already have a regular exercise program going, the time during which you're preparing for an exam is actually an excellent time to start one. And if you're already keeping fit—or trying to get that way—don't let the pressure of preparing for an exam fool you into quitting now. Exercise helps reduce stress by pumping wonderful, good-feeling hormones called endorphins into your system. It also increases the oxygen supply throughout your body, including your brain, so you'll be at peak performance on test day.

A half hour of vigorous activity—enough to raise a sweat—every day should be your aim. If you're really pressed for time, every other day is okay. Choose an activity you like and get out there and do it. Jogging with a friend always makes the time go faster, or take a radio.

But don't overdo it. You don't want to exhaust yourself. Moderation is the key.

Diet

First of all, cut out the junk. Go easy on caffeine and nicotine, and eliminate alcohol and any other drugs from your system at least two weeks before the exam. Promise yourself a binge the night after the exam, if need be.

What your body needs for peak performance is simply a balanced diet. Eat plenty of fruits and vegetables, along with protein and carbohydrates. Foods that are high in lecithin (an amino acid), such as fish and beans, are especially good "brain foods."

The night before the exam, you might "carbo-load" the way athletes do before a contest. Eat a big plate of spaghetti, rice and beans, or whatever your favorite carbohydrate is.

Rest

You probably know how much sleep you need every night to be at your best, even if you don't always get it. Make sure you do get that much sleep, though, for at least a week before the exam. Moderation is important here, too. Extra sleep will just make you groggy.

If you're not a morning person and your exam will be given in the morning, you should reset your internal clock so that your body doesn't think you're taking an exam at 3 A.M. You have to start this process well before the exam. The way it works is to get up half an hour earlier each morning, and then go to bed half an hour earlier that night. Don't try it the other way around; you'll just toss and turn if you go to bed early without having gotten up early. The next morning, get up another half an hour earlier, and so on. How long you will have to do this depends on how late you're used to getting up. Use the following Physical Preparation Checklist to make sure you're in tip-top form.

Physical Preparation Checklist

During the week before the test, write down 1) what physical exercise you engaged in and for how long and 2) what you ate for each meal. Remember, you're trying for at least half an hour of exercise every other day (preferably every day) and a balanced diet that's light on junk food.

Exam minus 7 days

Exercise: ______ for ______ minutes

Breakfast: ____________________

Lunch: ____________________

Dinner: ____________________

Snacks: ____________________

Exam minus 6 days

Exercise: ______ for ______ minutes

Breakfast: ____________________

Lunch: ____________________

Dinner: ____________________

Snacks: ____________________

Exam minus 5 days

Exercise: ______ for ______ minutes

Breakfast: ____________________

Lunch: ____________________

Dinner: ____________________

Snacks: ____________________

Exam minus 4 days

Exercise: ______ for ______ minutes

Breakfast: ____________________

Lunch: ____________________

Dinner: ____________________

Snacks: ____________________

Exam minus 3 days

Exercise: ______ for ______ minutes

Breakfast: ____________________

Lunch: ____________________

Dinner: ____________________

Snacks: ____________________

Exam minus 2 days

Exercise: ______ for ______ minutes

Breakfast: ____________________

Lunch: ____________________

Dinner: ____________________

Snacks: ____________________

Exam minus 1 day

Exercise: ______ for ______ minutes

Breakfast: ____________________

Lunch: ____________________

Dinner: ____________________

Snacks: ____________________

Step 8: Get Your Act Together

Time to complete: 10 minutes to read; time to complete will vary
Activity: Complete Final Preparations worksheet
You're in control of your mind and body; you're in charge of test anxiety, your preparation, and your test-taking strategies. Now it's time to take charge of external factors, like the testing site and the materials you need to take the exam.

Find Out Where the Test Is and Make a Trial Run

The testing agency or your cosmetology instructor will notify you when and where your exam is being held. Do you know how to get to the testing site? Do you know how long it will take to get there? If not, make a trial run, preferably on the same day of the week at the same time of day. Make note, on the Final Preparations worksheet on page 22, of the amount of time it will take you to get to the exam site. Plan on arriving 10–15 minutes early so you can get the lay of the land, use the bathroom, and calm down. Then, figure out how early you will have to get up that morning, and make sure you get up that early every day for a week before the exam.

Gather Your Materials

The night before the exam, lay out the clothes you will wear and the materials you have to bring with you to the exam. Plan on dressing in layers; you won't have any control over the temperature of the examination room. Have a sweater or jacket you can take off if it's warm. Use the checklist on the Final Preparations worksheet to help you pull together what you'll need.

Don't Skip Breakfast

Even if you don't usually eat breakfast, do so on exam morning. A cup of coffee doesn't count. Don't eat doughnuts or other sweet foods, either. A sugar high will leave you with a sugar low in the middle of the exam. A mix of protein and carbohydrates is best: Cereal with milk and just a little sugar, or eggs with toast, will do your body a world of good.

Step 9: Do It!

Time to complete: 10 minutes, plus test-taking time
Activity: Ace the Cosmetology Exam!
Fast forward to exam day. You're ready. You made a study plan and followed through. You practiced your test-taking strategies while working through this book. You're in control of your physical, mental, and emotional state. You know when and where to show up and what to bring with you. In other words, you're better prepared than most of the other people taking the Cosmetology Exam with you. You're psyched.

Just one more thing. When you're done with the exam, you will have earned a reward. Plan a celebration. Call up your friends and plan a party, or have a nice dinner for two—whatever your heart desires. Give yourself something to look forward to.

And then do it. Go into the exam, full of confidence, armed with test-taking strategies you've practiced until they're second nature. You're in control of yourself, your environment, and your performance on the exam. You're ready to succeed. So do it. Go in there and ace the exam. And look forward to your future career as a cosmetologist!

Final Preparations

Getting to the Exam Site

Location of exam site: ____________________

Date: ____________________

Departure time: ____________________

Do I know how to get to the exam site? Yes ___ No ___ (If no, make a trial run.)

Time it will take to get to exam site____________________

Things to Lay Out the Night Before

Clothes I will wear ___

Sweater/jacket ___

Watch ___

Photo ID ___

No. 2 pencils ___

__________ ___

__________ ___

LESSON

COSMETOLOGY PRACTICE EXAM 1

CHAPTER SUMMARY

This is the first of four practice exams based on the core content of your cosmetology coursework. Use this exam as a pretest. Like the other tests in this book, Exam 1 is based on the cosmetology subjects tested throughout the United States. See Lesson 1 for additional information on the exam.

Now that you have studied the LearningExpress Test Preparation System, you are ready to take Cosmetology Practice Exam 1. Most cosmetology exams are timed, but for now, don't worry about how long you take to answer the questions. Try to relax. You can practice under timed conditions with the other practice exams in this book.

The answer sheet is on the following page, followed by the exam. The correct answers, each fully explained, follow the exam. When you have read and understood all the answers, turn back to Lesson 1 for an explanation of how to score and analyze your exam. You will then determine possible weak areas to study further in Lesson 4, Cosmetology Refresher Course.

Practice Exam 1

1. a b c d
2. a b c d
3. a b c d
4. a b c d
5. a b c d
6. a b c d
7. a b c d
8. a b c d
9. a b c d
10. a b c d
11. a b c d
12. a b c d
13. a b c d
14. a b c d
15. a b c d
16. a b c d
17. a b c d
18. a b c d
19. a b c d
20. a b c d
21. a b c d
22. a b c d
23. a b c d
24. a b c d
25. a b c d
26. a b c d
27. a b c d
28. a b c d
29. a b c d
30. a b c d
31. a b c d
32. a b c d
33. a b c d
34. a b c d
35. a b c d
36. a b c d
37. a b c d
38. a b c d
39. a b c d
40. a b c d
41. a b c d
42. a b c d
43. a b c d
44. a b c d
45. a b c d
46. a b c d
47. a b c d
48. a b c d
49. a b c d
50. a b c d
51. a b c d
52. a b c d
53. a b c d
54. a b c d
55. a b c d
56. a b c d
57. a b c d
58. a b c d
59. a b c d
60. a b c d
61. a b c d
62. a b c d
63. a b c d
64. a b c d
65. a b c d
66. a b c d
67. a b c d
68. a b c d
69. a b c d
70. a b c d
71. a b c d
72. a b c d
73. a b c d
74. a b c d
75. a b c d
76. a b c d
77. a b c d
78. a b c d
79. a b c d
80. a b c d
81. a b c d
82. a b c d
83. a b c d
84. a b c d
85. a b c d
86. a b c d
87. a b c d
88. a b c d
89. a b c d
90. a b c d
91. a b c d
92. a b c d
93. a b c d
94. a b c d
95. a b c d
96. a b c d
97. a b c d
98. a b c d
99. a b c d
100. a b c d

Practice Exam 1

1. Before placing implements in a disinfecting solution, they should be
a. wiped with a towel.
b. rinsed with cold water.
c. wiped off with a tissue.
d. cleaned with warm soapy water.

2. What bonds in the hair are easily broken down by heat and water?
a. hydrogen bonds
b. salt bonds
c. disulfide bonds
d. peptide bonds

3. The best way to avoid back strain while working is to
a. position the client as low as possible.
b. keep your knees bent at a 90° angle.
c. keep your spine curved downward at all times.
d. maintain good posture and body alignment.

4. Good dental hygiene involves visiting the dentist twice each year and
a. brushing and flossing regularly.
b. copious use of breath mints.
c. drinking fluoridated water.
d. drinking lots of fluids.

5. Bacteria that do NOT cause disease are referred to as
a. parasitic.
b. nonpathogenic.
c. microbes.
d. saprophytes.

6. Disease-causing bacteria can be spread by
a. touching bacterial spores.
b. getting wet or cold.
c. cleaning with disinfectants.
d. coughing or spitting.

7. Which of the following is a contagious skin disease caused by a fungus?
a. scabies
b. tuberculosis
c. ringworm
d. AIDS

8. The method of cleaning instruments that kills all microorganisms, including bacterial spores, is
a. decontamination.
b. sanitation.
c. sterilization.
d. washing.

9. Antiseptics differ from disinfectants because they
a. kill bacterial spores.
b. can be used without government authorization.
c. are safe to use on skin.
d. require a prescription from a physician.

10. A quaternary ammonium compound is used as
a. a disinfectant.
b. an antiseptic.
c. a styptic.
d. a deodorant.

11. When using disinfectants, you should remember that they
a. kill all dangerous germs on contact.
b. cannot reach germs hidden in nooks and crannies.
c. can be dangerous if used incorrectly.
d. are inexpensive and, therefore, should be used liberally.

12. Trichology is the study of
a. hair.
b. beauty.
c. magic.
d. color.

13. Name the two distinct phases of the life cycle of bacteria.
a. preliminary and complete
b. vegetative and spore forming
c. fast and slow
d. infectious and noninfectious

14. Seen in cross section, straight hair would appear to be
a. round.
b. oval.
c. almost flat.
d. completely flat.

15. Your client has a bad case of dry dandruff. You should suggest
a. treatment by a doctor.
b. infrequent shampooing with regular soap.
c. scalp treatments and frequent mild shampoos.
d. ultraviolet treatments to the scalp.

16. Alopecia areata occurs when the client's hair
a. suddenly falls out in round patches.
b. changes from oily to very dry.
c. produces excessive amounts of sebum.
d. turns gray very suddenly.

17. The visible portion of the nail itself is referred to as the
a. nail plate.
b. nail bed.
c. free edge.
d. root.

18. A hangnail can be caused by
a. cutting the cuticle improperly.
b. too many hot-oil manicures.
c. injury to the nail bed.
d. fungus or bacterial infection.

19. One way to reassure clients about the cleanliness and sanitation of your implements is to
a. tell them that all implements are sterilized.
b. place the implements into a jar with disinfecting solution in it.
c. tell them no one has ever gotten an infection in your salon.
d. keep all implements in your pocket.

20. The outermost and thinnest layer of the skin is the
a. dermis.
b. epidermis.
c. papillary layer.
d. subcutaneous tissue.

21. The study of the skin and its diseases and treatment is referred to as
a. dermatology.
b. histology.
c. pathology.
d. trichology.

22. A steatoma, or sebaceous cyst, is
a. a chronic inflammation on the nose and cheeks.
b. a subcutaneous tumor of a sebaceous gland.
c. an accumulation of sebaceous matter beneath the skin.
d. a contagious disease of the sebaceous glands.

23. Which agency regulates how cosmetologists store, use, mix, and dispose of chemicals properly?
a. SGA
b. EPA
c. OSHA
d. FDA

24. Which is an example of a local infection?
a. measles
b. pimple or abscess
c. common cold
d. chicken pox

25. Which of the following lives only by penetrating cells and becoming part of them?
a. viruses
b. bacteria
c. organisms
d. amoebas

26. The main function of the blood is to
a. add color to the face and lips.
b. provide structure and support to body systems.
c. carry food and oxygen and eliminate wastes.
d. provide fluid to all the body tissues.

27. Which of the following substances will NOT conduct electricity?
a. the human body
b. silver
c. glass
d. copper

28. Which is the procedure for an indirect application of high-frequency current?
a. Hold one electrode while the client holds the other.
b. Hold the electrode while the client massages the treatment area.
c. Hold the electrode while massaging the client.
d. Massage the area to be treated while the client holds the electrode.

29. The chemical symbol for hydrogen peroxide is
a. H_2O.
b. H_2O_2.
c. H_2SO_4.
d. NaOH.

30. Surfactants are used to remove which of the following from the hair?
a. color
b. curl
c. oils
d. dryness

31. What happens in each individual hair shaft when an aniline derivative (oxidation) tint is mixed with hydrogen peroxide and applied?
- **a.** Heat is created, causing the hair to soften and absorb color.
- **b.** The cortex swells, allowing pigment molecules to enter.
- **c.** The H-bonds and S-bonds are broken, changing the hair's shape.
- **d.** The disulfide bonds are rebonded in waving lines.

32. Which type of nail cosmetic consists of the following ingredients: lanolin, petroleum, and beeswax?
- **a.** hand sanitizer
- **b.** nail bleach
- **c.** cuticle cream
- **d.** polish remover

33. Which would be the best location for a successful salon?
- **a.** your home on a quiet suburban street
- **b.** your home in an apartment building
- **c.** a single store in a residential neighborhood
- **d.** a mall that gets both car and foot traffic

34. In a corporation, each owner's liability is limited by the
- **a.** amount he or she has invested in the business.
- **b.** total amount the business is worth.
- **c.** amount of business insurance he or she purchases.
- **d.** amount of personal wealth he or she has amassed.

35. Which current of electricity is used for scalp and facial treatments because it increases blood flow, elimination and absorption, and metabolism, and has a germicidal effect when electrodes are used to apply it to the scalp and skin?
- **a.** faradic current
- **b.** Tesla high-frequency current
- **c.** sinusoidal current
- **d.** galvanic current

36. To be a successful cosmetologist in the salon business, you must be proficient as a hairstylist and a
- **a.** message therapist.
- **b.** counselor.
- **c.** driver.
- **d.** salesperson.

37. Before draping a client, you should do all of the following EXCEPT
- **a.** wash your hands.
- **b.** ask the client to wash his or her hands.
- **c.** ask the client to remove any necklaces.
- **d.** turn the client's collar in.

38. Why is it important to place a towel or neck strip under the cape between the client's skin and the cape when draping a client?
- **a.** to absorb sweat
- **b.** to cool the skin
- **c.** for sanitary reasons
- **d.** for fashionable reason

39. Besides cleaning the client's hair and scalp, a good shampoo can also
- **a.** change the color of a client's hair.
- **b.** change the texture of a client's hair.
- **c.** make the client's hair appear fuller and longer.
- **d.** give the client a good impression of the salon.

40. While shampooing a client, you would protect his or her face, neck, and ears from the water spray with
a. your hand.
b. the cape.
c. the neck strip.
d. your apron.

41. What type of shampoo should you use on chemically treated hair?
a. a mild shampoo
b. an acid-balanced shampoo
c. a shampoo for dry hair
d. a medicated shampoo

42. Dry shampoos are used only on clients
a. who are about to have a permanent.
b. who have chemically treated hair.
c. whose health does not permit shampoos.
d. who are particular about shampoos.

43. The muscle attached to a hair follicle is called the
a. corrugator muscle.
b. temporalis muscle.
c. masseter muscle.
d. arrector pili muscle.

44. A whitish discoloration of the nails caused by injury to the base of the nail is called
a. leukonychia.
b. melanonychia.
c. onychatrophia.
d. pterygium.

45. How can you use polish to give an elongated appearance to clubbed nails?
a. Leave the half moons at the bases unpolished.
b. Leave the tips of the nails unpolished.
c. Leave the sides of the nails unpolished.
d. Apply very bright polish to the entire nail.

46. The correct method for removing sculptured nails is to
a. clip them off with scissors.
b. file them off with an emery board.
c. apply a solvent and push them off.
d. use nail polish remover, as for regular polish.

47. A client who has athlete's foot requests a pedicure. You should
a. refer the client to a doctor for treatment.
b. treat the client with medicated powder and then give the pedicure.
c. use strict sanitary precautions to avoid spreading the infection.
d. give the pedicure as requested, no matter what.

48. All of the following are among the goals of a professional massage EXCEPT to
a. exercise muscles.
b. maintain muscle tone.
c. stimulate circulation.
d. get a good tip from the customer.

49. Kneading movements in massage therapy do all of the following EXCEPT
a. exercise the muscles.
b. give deep stimulation.
c. improve muscle tone.
d. improve circulation.

50. For sanitary reasons, you should always remove products such as facial creams from their containers with
a. your fingers.
b. a clean spatula.
c. a used teaspoon.
d. the client's fingers.

51. The correct method for applying cleansing cream is to start at the
a. forehead and work downward.
b. back and work upward.
c. cheeks and work in a circular fashion.
d. neck and work upward.

52. You can best help clients relax during facial manipulations by
a. talking to them continually.
b. having them visualize a relaxing scene.
c. maintaining an even rhythm and pressure.
d. telling them when you are about to start a new movement.

53. What effect on the skin would a mask of fresh strawberries have?
a. an astringent effect
b. a softening effect
c. a hydrating effect
d. It would clear impurities.

54. For a client with very light skin, you should choose a foundation that is
a. a shade lighter than the natural skin tone.
b. the same as the natural skin tone.
c. a shade darker than the natural skin tone.
d. a rosy shade.

55. The correct way to test the color of a foundation is to blend some of it on the client's
a. cheek.
b. nose.
c. jawline.
d. earlobe.

56. To create a natural look, you should apply cheek color no closer to the nose than the
a. outer corner of the eye.
b. center of the eye.
c. inner corner of the eye.
d. cheekbone.

57. The coloring agent used for lash and brow tint is
a. an aniline-derivative dye.
b. hydrogen peroxide.
c. lash- and brow-tinting solution.
d. semipermanent hair-color solution.

58. Why should a protective base be applied to the scalp prior to the application of a base relaxer?
a. to make the relaxer work faster
b. to straighten the hair more
c. to avoid chemical abrasions or sores on the scalp
d. to enhance the chemical process

59. In doing relaxers, which of the three strengths would be used on color-treated, damaged, or fine-textured hair?
a. super strength
b. regular strength
c. extra-mild strength
d. mild strength

60. In permanent waving, you have chemical and physical processes. Which of the following is not part of the physical process of permanent waving?
   a. draping
   b. waving lotion
   c. rodding hair
   d. shampooing hair

61. In order to determine what size partings or sections you will use, you must assess your client's hair in terms of
   a. length.
   b. porosity.
   c. color.
   d. density.

62. Hair should be shampooed and left moist before
   a. wrapping.
   b. draping.
   c. leaving.
   d. relaxing.

63. How many towels are used to drape for chemical texture services?
   a. one
   b. two
   c. three
   d. four

64. The correct procedure for applying most neutralizers is to
   a. apply, wait 15 minutes, repeat, remove rods.
   b. apply, rinse, repeat, remove rods.
   c. apply, repeat, wait five minutes, remove rods.
   d. remove rods, apply, rinse, repeat.

65. Ideal conditions for a hair-color consultation include
   a. natural lighting and neutral background colors.
   b. fluorescent lighting and bright background colors.
   c. incandescent lighting and warm background colors.
   d. very low lighting and a black background.

66. Warm-toned colors are made up primarily of
   a. blues and greens.
   b. reds and yellows.
   c. black and white.
   d. shades of gray.

67. Clients who have their hair colored usually visit the salon
   a. every three to five weeks.
   b. every five to nine weeks.
   c. every four to 12 weeks.
   d. every five to 15 weeks.

68. A primary color is one that is a pure or fundamental color that cannot
   a. be seen in the light.
   b. be seen in the dark.
   c. be achieved from a mixture.
   d. be mixed with secondary colors.

69. A highlighting shampoo is a mixture of shampoo and
   a. hydrogen peroxide.
   b. ammonium nitrate.
   c. aniline-derivative tint.
   d. cream rinse.

70. Your client has requested a return to her darker, natural hair color. In order to smooth out the line of demarcation between the two shades, you should use a
- a. filler followed by a soap cap.
- b. two-step lightening process.
- c. complementary tint.
- d. color remover.

71. Your client will be most likely to accept your suggestions about hair color and hair-color services when you
- a. begin by explaining the price of all your services.
- b. base your suggestions on the client's needs and lifestyle.
- c. carefully explain the underlying chemistry of hair coloring.
- d. show the client color photos of movie stars with the same color.

72. Colorists use the Level System to analyze hair color's
- a. lightness or darkness.
- b. shininess or drabness.
- c. brightness or dimness.
- d. wetness or dryness.

73. Which is a benefit of knowing the laws of color?
- a. to learn your colors
- b. to formulate the client's desired color
- c. to enhance a client's natural eye and skin color
- d. to match a client's original hair color

74. Which of the following is NOT a category of hair-coloring product?
- a. accelerator
- b. temporary
- c. semipermanent
- d. permanent

75. Which of these hair-color services does NOT require a patch test before application?
- a. demipermanent
- b. temporary
- c. semipermanent
- d. permanent

76. Which of the following should be done before lightening a client's hair?
- a. Analyze the neckline.
- b. Brush the hair vigorously.
- c. Perform a strand test.
- d. Apply protective cream to the scalp.

77. In general, the greater the concentration of sodium hydroxide in a hair-relaxing formula, the
- a. quicker the chemical reaction and the greater the danger of hair damage.
- b. quicker the chemical reaction and the lesser the danger of hair damage.
- c. slower the chemical reaction and the greater the danger of hair damage.
- d. slower the chemical reaction and the lesser the danger of hair damage.

78. What type of shampoo should be used after an application of sodium hydroxide relaxer?
- a. conditioning shampoo
- b. alkaline shampoo
- c. neutralizing shampoo
- d. normal shampoo

79. A chemical blowout is a combination of
- **a.** chemical hair relaxing and a cold permanent wave.
- **b.** chemical hair relaxing and styling.
- **c.** ammonium thioglycolate (“thio”) and sodium hydroxide relaxing.
- **d.** chemical hair relaxing and a soft-curl permanent.

80. How many pairs of cranial nerves are there?
- **a.** 8
- **b.** 10
- **c.** 12
- **d.** 16

81. To save time, both the comb and shears should be held in your dominant hand while you are
- **a.** styling hair.
- **b.** blow-drying hair.
- **c.** combing hair.
- **d.** cutting hair.

82. Which of these reference points is NOT commonly used by hairstylists?
- **a.** ears
- **b.** jawline
- **c.** occipital bone
- **d.** lip line

83. Which statement about use of the razor for haircutting is incorrect?
- **a.** The razor guard should face you, the cosmetologist, while you use the razor.
- **b.** The razor can be used for thinning as well as for haircutting.
- **c.** When combing the hair, put the razor down and hold the comb in your right hand.
- **d.** Keep the hair damp while working, to prevent dulling the blade of the razor.

84. On which part of the human body is the skin thinnest?
- **a.** palms
- **b.** soles
- **c.** eyelids
- **d.** eyebrows

85. In terms of braiding and other natural hairstyling, what does texture refer to?
- **a.** the diameter of the hair
- **b.** the feel of the hair
- **c.** wave pattern
- **d.** all of the above

86. To emphasize the ridge in a finger wave, you would press the ridge
- **a.** between your fingers.
- **b.** against the comb.
- **c.** against the head.
- **d.** between the fingers and the comb.

87. To remove tangles from hair before hairstyling, you should start combing at the
- **a.** forehead.
- **b.** crown.
- **c.** back of the head.
- **d.** nape of the neck.

88. Which of the following describes the process in which natural textured hair is intertwined and meshed together to form a style or separate network of hair?
- **a.** hair locking
- **b.** hair stepping
- **c.** hair meshing
- **d.** hair winding

89. Why are patch tests required before the application of hair extensions with bonding adhesive?
a. to check for durability
b. to check for allergic reactions
c. to check the density of the hair
d. to test the porosity of hair

90. A small wig used to cover the top or crown of the head only is referred to as a
a. fall.
b. wig.
c. hairpiece.
d. hair extension.

91. The best way to determine if a strand of hair is synthetic product or real human hair is to
a. immerse it in cold water.
b. burn it.
c. immerse it in alcohol.
d. freeze it.

92. Which of the following are hairlike projections that cause bacteria to move and are also known as cilia?
a. flagella
b. bacilli
c. spirilla
d. parasites

93. To avoid burning the client during thermal waving, you should
a. hold the comb between the scalp and iron.
b. keep the hair very wet.
c. always use a curling gel or lotion.
d. keep your fingers wrapped around the iron.

94. A long woven strip of hair that is sewn to elastic strips in a circular pattern to fit the head shape is called a
a. weft.
b. capless.
c. deft.
d. cap-on.

95. Which statement about setting and styling a wig is incorrect?
a. You must devise a style that conceals the hairline.
b. You should always set the wig while it is on the client.
c. You need to consider the added fullness of the client's hair and the wig's foundation.
d. You should use pin curls instead of rollers all around the hairline.

96. What percentage of the curl is removed by a soft press?
a. 30–40%
b. 40–50%
c. 50–60%
d. 60–70%

97. When performing a thermal straightening treatment, which should be applied to the hair just before treatment?
a. water
b. setting gel
c. pressing oil
d. shampoo

98. What is a protein fiber that composes the hair and nails?
a. melanin
b. tactile corpuscles
c. keratin
d. dermal

99. Hair color that lightens and deposits color in the hair shaft requires
a. two-process.
b. two-step.
c. single-process.
d. aniline.

100. Salaries and commissions (including payroll taxes) will account for what percentage of your total expenses?
a. 25.6%
b. 48.2%
c. 53.5%
d. 69.7%

Answers

1. d. Implements should be cleaned with warm, soapy water before they are placed in a disinfecting solution.
2. a. Hydrogen bonds in the hair are the physical bonds that are weak and can be broken with heat and water. They account for $\frac{1}{3}$ of the hair's strength.
3. d. Maintaining good posture and body alignment will help you avoid back strain.
4. a. Good dental hygiene involves visiting the dentist twice each year as well as brushing and flossing regularly.
5. b. Nonpathogenic bacteria are those that do not cause disease.
6. d. Sneezing, coughing, spitting, and sharing personal articles such as combs and cosmetics are some of the ways in which diseases are spread.
7. c. Ringworm is a contagious skin disease that is caused by a fungus.
8. c. Sterilization, which is done in hospitals and doctors' offices, kills all microorganisms, including spores.
9. c. Antiseptics are safe to use on the skin.
10. a. Quaternary ammonium compound, more commonly called quat, is a blue disinfectant solution that is fast acting (5–15 minutes), nontoxic, odorless, and comes in a hospital-grade disinfecting formula, which is required by most state boards of cosmetology.
11. c. Disinfectants are powerful chemicals that can be dangerous if used incorrectly.
12. a. Trichology is the study of hair.
13. b. The life cycle of bacteria is made up of two distinct phases: the active or vegetative stage and the inactive or spore-forming stage.
14. a. In cross section, straight hair is round.
15. c. Scalp treatments and frequent mild shampoos will benefit a client with dry dandruff.
16. a. Alopecia areata refers to a condition in which the client's hair falls out suddenly in round patches.
17. a. The nail plate is the visible portion of the nail.
18. a. A hangnail, or split cuticle, can be caused by improper cutting or removal of the cuticle.
19. b. Wipe off the implement and place it in your jar with disinfecting solution in it. This reassures the client as they *see* you are disinfecting all implements and tools after use.
20. b. The epidermis is the outermost layer of the skin.
21. a. The study of the skin and its diseases and treatment is dermatology.
22. b. A steatoma, or sebaceous cyst, is a tumor of a sebaceous gland.
23. c. OSHA, Occupational Safety and Health Administration, is part of the U.S. Department of Labor. Its job is to regulate and enforce safety in a place of work. If there are violations, a fee is imposed on the salon.
24. a. A local infection, such as a pimple or abscess, is one that is confined to a particular part of the body and is indicated by a lesion containing pus.
25. a. Viruses live only by penetrating cells and becoming part of them, while bacteria are organisms that can live on their own. Viruses cause respiratory and digestive tract infections, as well as the common cold, hepatitis, HIV, chicken pox, measles, etc.
26. c. The blood carries nutrients and oxygen to all body cells; it also carries wastes away from the cells.
27. c. Familiar nonconductors include glass, dry wood, plastic, and rubber.
28. d. This is the correct procedure for indirect application.
29. b. The symbol means that each molecule of hydrogen peroxide contains two atoms of hydrogen and two atoms of oxygen.

30. c. Surfactants are used to remove oils from the hair. Knowledge of the characteristics of surfactants will help you choose the best shampoo for each client's hair needs.

31. b. The alkaline chemical reaction causes the cortex to swell so that pigment molecules can permanently enter the hair shaft.

32. c. Cuticle creams have a base of lanolin, petroleum, or beeswax to correct or prevent dry cuticles and brittle nails, and can be used on a daily basis.

33. d. This location would result in the largest number of potential customers.

34. a. In a corporation, each stockholder (owner) can lose only the amount he or she has invested.

35. b. Tesla high-frequency current is commonly used for scalp and facial treatments. Electrodes are used in a handheld machine and applied directly to the skin and scalp. It is commonly called the "violet ray" because the current is purple, or violet, in the tube when applied. Effects are either soothing or stimulating depending on method of application. During scalp treatments, the cosmetologist can use the indirection method in which scalp manipulations are applied while the client holds the electrode.

36. d. Selling products to clients is an increasingly important part of the salon business.

37. b. It is not necessary for the client to wash his or her hands before draping.

38. c. For sanitary reasons, always place a towel or neck strip between the cape and the client's skin.

39. d. Because the shampoo sets the stage for the client's entire visit, a good shampoo can help give a favorable impression.

40. a. Use your free hand to protect the client's face, neck, and ears from the water.

41. a. Because chemically treated hair can be fragile, use a mild shampoo.

42. c. Dry shampoos are used only on clients whose health forbids shampoos.

43. d. The arrector pili muscle is attached to the hair follicle and reacts to heat and cold, causing goose bumps.

44. a. Leukonychia is a whitish discoloration of the nails, caused by injury to the base of the nail.

45. c. Leaving the sides unpolished makes the nails look more slender.

46. c. Apply the special solvent provided and then gently push the acrylic nails off with an orangewood stick.

47. a. Do not treat clients with contagious skin conditions; refer them to a physician for treatment.

48. d. The goals of professional massage services are to exercise muscles, maintain muscle tone, and stimulate circulation.

49. a. Kneading movements give deep stimulation to the muscles and other tissue; they improve muscle tone and circulation.

50. b. Always use a clean spatula, not your fingers, to remove products from their container.

51. d. When applying cleansing cream, start at the neck and work upward.

52. c. The best way to induce relaxation during a massage is to maintain even pressure and rhythm.

53. a. Fresh strawberries would have an astringent effect.

54. b. The same as the natural skin tone.

55. c. Test the color of a foundation by blending a small amount on the client's jawline.

56. b. Apply cheek color from the center of the eye outward.

57. c. Do not use any tinting solution, or coloring agent, not specifically intended for lashes and brows.

58. c. A base relaxer is a sodium hydroxide relaxer that requires you to apply a protective base to the scalp first to avoid chemical abrasions or sores on the scalp.

59. d. Mild-strength sodium hydroxide relaxer would be formulated to use on color-treated, damaged, or fine-textured hair because of the lower concentration of hydroxide.

60. a. Draping a client is NOT part of the physical process of permanent waving.

61. d. The density of the hair determines the size of the partings, or sections, you will use.

62. a. Hair should be shampooed and left moist—but not saturated with water—before wrapping.

63. b. Two towels should be used to drape for a chemical texture service to absorb accidental spills.

64. c. The correct procedure is given.

65. a. Natural lighting and a neutral background will show colors in their truest appearance.

66. b. Warm-toned colors are those in which reds and yellows predominate.

67. c. Depending on the color service and the rate of hair growth, most clients who have their hair colored usually visit the salon every four to 12 weeks.

68. c. Primary colors are pure or fundamental colors that cannot be achieved from a mixture. The primary colors are blue, red, and yellow.

69. a. A highlighting shampoo that contains hydrogen peroxide will lighten the natural hair color slightly.

70. a. Use a filler, followed by a soap cap, to smooth out the line between the two shades.

71. b. Your client is most likely to accept the services you suggest when you base them on an analysis of his or her personal needs and lifestyle.

72. a. Colorists use the Level System to analyze the lightness or darkness of a hair color. Hair-color levels are arranged on a scale of 1 to 10, with 1 being the darkest and 10 being the lightest.

73. b. The laws of color will enable you to mix and formulate colors to achieve the desired effect.

74. a. An accelerator is a product that is added to bleach to make it work more quickly.

75. b. All hair-color products, except for temporary color, require a patch test before application to determine if the client is allergic to the product.

76. c. Perform a strand test before lightening a client's hair.

77. a. The greater the concentration of sodium hydroxide, the quicker the chemical reaction and the greater the risk of hair damage.

78. c. After all traces of the relaxer are rinsed out of the hair, shampoo three times with a neutralizing shampoo recommended by the manufacturer. On the third shampoo, leave in the hair for five minutes and rinse thoroughly. Follow the manufacturer's directions.

79. b. A chemical blowout procedure combines chemical hair relaxing with hairstyling.

80. c. There are 12 pairs of cranial nerves that originate in the brain and reach various parts of the head, face, and neck.

81. c. To save time, keep both the scissors and comb in your right hand while combing the hair.

82. d. The most commonly used reference points in haircutting are the ears, jawline, and the occipital bone, or apex.

83. c. Keep both the razor and the comb in your right hand.

84. c. Eyelids are the thinnest skin on the body. Palms and soles are the thickest.

85. d. Texture refers to the diameter of the hair (whether the hair is coarse, medium, or fine), the feel (whether the hair feels oily, dry, hard, soft, smooth, coarse, or wiry), and the wave pattern (whether the hair is straight, wavy, curly, or coiled).

86. a. Press the ridge between your fingers while holding the fingers against the head.

87. d. Begin combing at the nape of the neck, a small section at a time, to remove tangles.

88. a. Hair locking, also called dreadlocks, is natural textured hair that is intertwined and meshed together to form a single or separate network of hair.

89. b. Bonding adhesive requires a patch test before application, as the client could have an allergic reaction to the adhesive.

90. c. If a hair addition does not fully cover the head, it is classified as a hairpiece, which is a small wig used to cover the top or crown of the head.

91. b. To find out if the hair is human or synthetic, pull a strand out of the wig or hairpiece and burn it with a match—human hair will burn slowly, giving off a distinctive odor, and a synthetic fiber will either "ball up" and melt or continue to flame and burn out very quickly, but will not give off an odor.

92. a. Flagella or cilia are hairlike projections that cause movement of bacteria. Bacilli and spirilla have these.

93. a. To avoid burning the client, always keep the comb between the scalp and the iron.

94. a. A weft is a long woven strip of hair that is sewn to elastic strips in a circular pattern to fit the head shape and is most used in the art of hair extensions to add artificial length to the natural hair.

95. b. Wigs are set and styled while on the blocking.

96. c. The soft press removes approximately 50–60% of the curl.

97. c. Pressing oil or cream is applied just before thermal straightening.

98. c. Keratin is the protein that composes the hair and nails.

99. c. Single process lightens and deposits a single process or single application.

100. c. Salaries and commissions (including payroll taxes) will be your biggest expense and will account for 53.5% of your total expenses.

LESSON

COSMETOLOGY REFRESHER COURSE

LESSON SUMMARY

This chapter is a 250-question review, divided into content areas like those found on typical state board of cosmetology exams. Use this Refresher Course as a study aid rather than as a timed test.

NOW THAT YOU have taken the first practice exam, you should have some idea of what areas you need to work on. This Refresher Course is conveniently divided into content areas like those on the cosmetology exams in this book, but in this lesson, there are headings that indicate the content areas:

Scientific Concepts

Nutrition/Ergonomics, questions 1–5
Your Professional Image, questions 6, 7
Infection Control and Federal Regulations, questions 8–12
Cells, Tissue, and Body Systems, questions 13–20
Bacteriology, questions 21–29
Decontamination and Infection Control, questions 30–38
Properties of the Hair and Scalp, questions 39–49
The Nail and Its Disorders, questions 50–56
The Skin and Its Disorders, questions 57–64
Cells, Anatomy, and Physiology, questions 65–72

Electricity and Light Therapy, questions 73–82
Chemistry, questions 83–90
The Salon Business, questions 91–102

Physical Services

Draping, questions 103–108
Shampooing, Rinsing, and Conditioning, questions 109–116
Manicuring and Pedicuring, questions 117–122
Advanced Nail Techniques, questions 123–132
Theory of Massage, questions 133–137
Facials, questions 138–146
Facial Makeup, questions 147–153
Hair Removal, questions 154–160

Chemical Services

Permanent Waving, questions 161–170
Hair Coloring, questions 171–197
Chemical Hair Relaxing, questions 198–204

Hair Design

Haircutting, questions 205–217
Hairstyling, questions 218–232
Thermal Hair Straightening, questions 233–237
Braiding and Braid Extensions, questions 238–245
Wigs and Hair Enhancements, questions 246–250

While this review is written in the same multiple-choice format as the actual Cosmetology Exam, do not time yourself or grade your results. Instead, use this lesson—along with your textbook, course notes, and materials—to refresh your memory of the core content of your cosmetology classes. Your results on the first practice exam have shown you which areas you need to review most intensely, so you may want to start with the subjects that gave you the most trouble. Another strategy is to work through the entire lesson, in order, for an overall review.

One tactic that will make your review more useful is to select the best answer to each question and think of an explanation to support further why you find this to be the best choice. Next, look at the answer key that follows each subject area. Uncover each answer explanation, one at a time, in the key. Then, compare your explanation for the answer you chose with the answer explanation given. In this way, you can review your subject while reinforcing the correct choices you made and immediately correcting the wrong choices you might have made.

An answer sheet you can use to record your answers is on the next two pages. Remember, though, that you should not treat this review like a test. Tackling only one or two subject areas at a time will help you remember what you are learning. The answer sheet is just a convenient place to put your answers. You may prefer simply to circle the correct answer in the book.

Refresher Course

1.	a	b	c	d
2.	a	b	c	d
3.	a	b	c	d
4.	a	b	c	d
5.	a	b	c	d
6.	a	b	c	d
7.	a	b	c	d
8.	a	b	c	d
9.	a	b	c	d
10.	a	b	c	d
11.	a	b	c	d
12.	a	b	c	d
13.	a	b	c	d
14.	a	b	c	d
15.	a	b	c	d
16.	a	b	c	d
17.	a	b	c	d
18.	a	b	c	d
19.	a	b	c	d
20.	a	b	c	d
21.	a	b	c	d
22.	a	b	c	d
23.	a	b	c	d
24.	a	b	c	d
25.	a	b	c	d
26.	a	b	c	d
27.	a	b	c	d
28.	a	b	c	d
29.	a	b	c	d
30.	a	b	c	d
31.	a	b	c	d
32.	a	b	c	d
33.	a	b	c	d
34.	a	b	c	d
35.	a	b	c	d
36.	a	b	c	d
37.	a	b	c	d
38.	a	b	c	d
39.	a	b	c	d
40.	a	b	c	d
41.	a	b	c	d
42.	a	b	c	d
43.	a	b	c	d
44.	a	b	c	d
45.	a	b	c	d
46.	a	b	c	d
47.	a	b	c	d
48.	a	b	c	d
49.	a	b	c	d
50.	a	b	c	d
51.	a	b	c	d
52.	a	b	c	d
53.	a	b	c	d
54.	a	b	c	d
55.	a	b	c	d
56.	a	b	c	d
57.	a	b	c	d
58.	a	b	c	d
59.	a	b	c	d
60.	a	b	c	d
61.	a	b	c	d
62.	a	b	c	d
63.	a	b	c	d
64.	a	b	c	d
65.	a	b	c	d
66.	a	b	c	d
67.	a	b	c	d
68.	a	b	c	d
69.	a	b	c	d
70.	a	b	c	d
71.	a	b	c	d
72.	a	b	c	d
73.	a	b	c	d
74.	a	b	c	d
75.	a	b	c	d
76.	a	b	c	d
77.	a	b	c	d
78.	a	b	c	d
79.	a	b	c	d
80.	a	b	c	d
81.	a	b	c	d
82.	a	b	c	d
83.	a	b	c	d
84.	a	b	c	d
85.	a	b	c	d
86.	a	b	c	d
87.	a	b	c	d
88.	a	b	c	d
89.	a	b	c	d
90.	a	b	c	d
91.	a	b	c	d
92.	a	b	c	d
93.	a	b	c	d
94.	a	b	c	d
95.	a	b	c	d
96.	a	b	c	d
97.	a	b	c	d
98.	a	b	c	d
99.	a	b	c	d
100.	a	b	c	d
101.	a	b	c	d
102.	a	b	c	d
103.	a	b	c	d
104.	a	b	c	d
105.	a	b	c	d
106.	a	b	c	d
107.	a	b	c	d
108.	a	b	c	d
109.	a	b	c	d
110.	a	b	c	d
111.	a	b	c	d
112.	a	b	c	d
113.	a	b	c	d
114.	a	b	c	d
115.	a	b	c	d
116.	a	b	c	d
117.	a	b	c	d
118.	a	b	c	d
119.	a	b	c	d
120.	a	b	c	d
121.	a	b	c	d
122.	a	b	c	d
123.	a	b	c	d
124.	a	b	c	d
125.	a	b	c	d
126.	a	b	c	d
127.	a	b	c	d
128.	a	b	c	d
129.	a	b	c	d
130.	a	b	c	d
131.	a	b	c	d
132.	a	b	c	d
133.	a	b	c	d
134.	a	b	c	d
135.	a	b	c	d

(over)

COSMETOLOGY ANSWER SHEET

Refresher Course (continued)

136. a b c d
137. a b c d
138. a b c d
139. a b c d
140. a b c d
141. a b c d
142. a b c d
143. a b c d
144. a b c d
145. a b c d
146. a b c d
147. a b c d
148. a b c d
149. a b c d
150. a b c d
151. a b c d
152. a b c d
153. a b c d
154. a b c d
155. a b c d
156. a b c d
157. a b c d
158. a b c d
159. a b c d
160. a b c d
161. a b c d
162. a b c d
163. a b c d
164. a b c d
165. a b c d
166. a b c d
167. a b c d
168. a b c d
169. a b c d
170. a b c d
171. a b c d
172. a b c d
173. a b c d
174. a b c d
175. a b c d
176. a b c d
177. a b c d
178. a b c d
179. a b c d
180. a b c d
181. a b c d
182. a b c d
183. a b c d
184. a b c d
185. a b c d
186. a b c d
187. a b c d
188. a b c d
189. a b c d
190. a b c d
191. a b c d
192. a b c d
193. a b c d
194. a b c d
195. a b c d
196. a b c d
197. a b c d
198. a b c d
199. a b c d
200. a b c d
201. a b c d
202. a b c d
203. a b c d
204. a b c d
205. a b c d
206. a b c d
207. a b c d
208. a b c d
209. a b c d
210. a b c d
211. a b c d
212. a b c d
213. a b c d
214. a b c d
215. a b c d
216. a b c d
217. a b c d
218. a b c d
219. a b c d
220. a b c d
221. a b c d
222. a b c d
223. a b c d
224. a b c d
225. a b c d
226. a b c d
227. a b c d
228. a b c d
229. a b c d
230. a b c d
231. a b c d
232. a b c d
233. a b c d
234. a b c d
235. a b c d
236. a b c d
237. a b c d
238. a b c d
239. a b c d
240. a b c d
241. a b c d
242. a b c d
243. a b c d
244. a b c d
245. a b c d
246. a b c d
247. a b c d
248. a b c d
249. a b c d
250. a b c d

Scientific Concepts

Nutrition/Ergonomics

1. Good posture means that your spine should be
a. straight.
b. bent.
c. curved.
d. swayed from back to front.

2. To maintain good posture while seated, you should rest most of your body weight on your
a. hips.
b. thighs.
c. buttocks.
d. knees.

3. What is the study of human characteristics related to specific work environments?
a. physical presentation
b. posture
c. ergonomics
d. professional image

4. Cosmetologists are subject to many physical injuries classified as MSDs. What does MSD stand for?
a. muscular diseases
b. manual diseases
c. microskeletal disorders
d. musculoskeletal disorders

5. Which one of the following is NOT a principle of ergonomics?
a. tilting the client's head so you can work without strain
b. adjusting the height of the chair for a comfortable working level
c. gripping and squeezing implements too tightly
d. placing one foot on a stool when standing for long periods of time

Your Professional Image

6. ____________________ is the practice of maintaining daily cleanliness, such as bathing, brushing and flossing teeth, and using mouthwash and deodorant to prevent offensive odors.
a. Personal grooming
b. Personal hygiene
c. Professional image
d. Professional presentation

7. Which of the following are NOT good nutrition habits?
a. eating plenty of fruits and vegetables
b. drinking plenty of water to stay hydrated and flush toxins
c. eating plenty of sugar and fats and drinking alcohol
d. eating whole-grain foods rather than refined or processed foods

Infection Control and Federal Regulations

8. How often should the shampoo bowl be disinfected?
a. once an hour
b. every five minutes
c. after each client
d. at the end of the day

9. What should be used at the end of the day to thoroughly disinfect a whirlpool pedicure chair (or throne)?
a. 20% chlorine bleach to a gallon of water
b. 5% chlorine bleach to a gallon of water
c. 70% alcohol to a gallon of water
d. 50% chlorine bleach to a gallon of water

10. What should be done to properly disinfect the pedicure foot spa after each client?
a. Rinse it with hot water.
b. Wipe it with a clean towel.
c. Rinse it with water, then dry it.
d. Clean it with hospital-grade disinfectant.

11. All products used in the salon are required by federal law to have an information sheet called a(n)
a. MSDS.
b. MSSD.
c. OSHA.
d. EPA.

12. Sterilizing can only be performed on what type of surfaces?
a. porous
b. nonporous
c. hard surfaces
d. soft surfaces

Cells, Tissue, and Body Systems

13. How should massage movements be applied to skin when massaging a muscle?
a. origin to insertion
b. up and down
c. back and forth
d. insertion to origin

14. Otology is the study of
a. nerves.
b. eyes.
c. ears.
d. bones.

15. The basic unit of all living matter is known as a
a. cell.
b. tissue.
c. catabolism.
d. system.

16. What is the largest organ of the body?
a. heart
b. stomach
c. liver
d. skin

17. What is the average heartbeat per minute?
a. 72–80
b. 60–70
c. 80–100
d. 100–120

18. The study of the functions of the body is known as
a. histology.
b. physiology.
c. anatomy.
d. bacteriology.

19. Which cranial nerve is the largest?
a. fifth
b. seventh
c. nasal
d. cervical

20. How many systems is the body composed of?
a. 8
b. 9
c. 10
d. 11

Bacteriology

21. Which of the following is NOT one of the body's defenses against infection?
a. unbroken skin
b. white blood cells
c. red blood cells
d. digestive juices

22. A person who is immune to a disease yet can transmit the disease to others is known as a
a. carrier.
b. vector.
c. antitoxin.
d. parasite.

23. Which of the following diseases is caused by a fungus?
a. ringworm
b. scabies
c. pediculosis
d. HIV

24. Which of the following ways can a cosmetologist create a risk of HIV infection in a salon?
a. using unsanitary implements
b. sneezing and coughing
c. sharing coffee cups or food
d. shaking hands or kissing

25. What is the most common pus-forming bacteria?
a. staphylococci
b. streptococci
c. tetanus bacilli
d. typhoid bacilli

26. Your client tells you that he has a disease on his scalp and asks you to treat it by shampooing his hair in very hot water. You should
a. comply with his request.
b. ask him to sign a form that states that you are not responsible if he is burned by the hot water.
c. refer the client to a physician for treatment.
d. contact the health department for information on how to treat this skin disease.

27. Nonpathogenic organisms perform which function?
a. decomposing garbage
b. decomposing soil fertility
c. maintaining food enzymes
d. promoting infectious microorganisms

28. What shape are the spirilla bacteria?
a. round
b. square
c. rod-shaped
d. corkscrew

29. How do cocci bacteria move about?
a. swim through water
b. through the air
c. with a flagella
d. on the backs of animals

Decontamination and Infection Control

30. Which statement about disinfection is correct?
a. Disinfectants should not be used on skin, hair, or nails.
b. Disinfectants destroy all microorganisms, including bacterial spores.
c. Disinfectants should be used only by health-care professionals.
d. Disinfectants are never used in salons.

31. The most important rule for using disinfectants safely is to always
a. obtain the necessary government permit before using.
b. read and follow the directions.
c. ask clients' permission before using.
d. wear a mask.

32. Before placing instruments and equipment in a disinfecting solution, you should
- a. wash your hands.
- b. clean them thoroughly.
- c. wipe them off.
- d. examine them carefully.

33. What is quat?
- a. an effective and fast-acting disinfectant
- b. a steam sterilization device
- c. an autoclave
- d. a solution of alcohol, bleach, and disinfectant

34. When using disinfectants, you should always
- a. wear rubber gloves and goggles.
- b. pour a small amount on your hands first.
- c. use a glass measuring cup to pour from.
- d. disinfect rubber items first.

35. Which statement about salon sanitation is correct?
- a. Sanitation can be maintained by regular weekly washing of floors, countertops, and instruments.
- b. Sanitation should be a full-time job of a health professional.
- c. Sanitation means cleaning every item in the salon correctly and regularly.
- d. Sanitation is important only to impress clients.

36. The proper procedure for disinfecting a countertop is to
- a. wipe with disinfectant solution, then with plain water, then with disinfectant again, and air dry.
- b. wipe once with disinfectant only.
- c. apply disinfectant with a cloth or sponge that has been sterilized in an autoclave and wipe dry with another cloth.
- d. clean with a cleaner, apply disinfectant, and follow the manufacturer's instructions.

37. To be an effective disinfectant, ethyl alcohol must be used in a solution of at least
- a. 40%.
- b. 50%.
- c. 60%.
- d. 70%.

38. You should change the solution used in a wet sanitizer
- a. every other day.
- b. twice a week.
- c. every day.
- d. when it starts to become cloudy.

Properties of the Hair and Scalp

39. Which of the following influences the health of a person's hair the most?
- a. economic success
- b. choice of cosmetologist
- c. physical and emotional health
- d. choice of shampoo rinse

40. A cowlick occurs when
- a. a tuft of hair stands straight up.
- b. a part of the hair is a different color from the rest.
- c. the hair growth forms a circular pattern.
- d. the hair parts naturally in the middle.

41. The hair cuticle is the
- **a.** outermost layer, composed of overlapping sheets of transparent protective cells.
- **b.** middle pigmented layer, composed of a fibrous material made up of elongated cells.
- **c.** innermost layer, also referred to as the pith.
- **d.** follicle from which the hair shaft emerges.

42. The purpose of scalp manipulations is to relieve tension and
- **a.** impress the client.
- **b.** clean the scalp.
- **c.** stimulate the scalp.
- **d.** relax the hair shafts.

43. The treatment for split ends is to
- **a.** apply oil treatments.
- **b.** shampoo frequently.
- **c.** keep the hair very long.
- **d.** use antidandruff shampoo.

44. A boil is
- **a.** a symptom of head louse infestation.
- **b.** a sign that the client is about to lose his or her hair.
- **c.** a result of severe oily dandruff.
- **d.** an acute infection of a hair follicle.

45. Which statement about head louse infestation is incorrect?
- **a.** The small white eggs, or nits, attach to individual hair shafts.
- **b.** A client with a head lice infestation can be safely treated in the salon.
- **c.** Head lice are treated with scalp medication and medicated shampoo.
- **d.** Head lice can be spread through contact with infested combs and hats.

46. The part of the hair that attaches directly to the papilla is called the
- **a.** follicle.
- **b.** epidermis.
- **c.** arrector pili muscle.
- **d.** bulb.

47. What determines the direction of hair growth?
- **a.** shape of the hair follicle
- **b.** thickness of the scalp
- **c.** cross-sectional shape of the hair shaft
- **d.** health of the skin and hair

48. Approximately how many hairs does the average person shed per day?
- **a.** 25–35
- **b.** 50
- **c.** 35–40
- **d.** 200 or more

49. The three hair shapes are round, almost flat, and
- **a.** square.
- **b.** oval.
- **c.** half moon.
- **d.** rectangular.

The Nail and Its Disorders

50. A normal, healthy nail grows
- **a.** from the free edge and over the tip of the finger.
- **b.** from the matrix and over the tip of the finger.
- **c.** from the free edge and back toward the half moon.
- **d.** from the lanula and back over the eponychium.

51. Which statement about nail growth is correct?
- a. Older people's nails grow more slowly than younger people's.
- b. The rate of nail growth is greatest in the winter.
- c. A person's state of health does not influence nail growth.
- d. Toenails grow more quickly than fingernails.

52. A nail that has been lost because of disease is likely to grow back
- a. black.
- b. distorted.
- c. reddened.
- d. normally.

53. If a client is accidentally cut during nail care, you should
- a. call an ambulance.
- b. offer to pay for HIV testing.
- c. apply antiseptic and a sterile bandage.
- d. drive the client to the doctor immediately.

54. A condition caused by injury to the nail or some disease or imbalance in the body is called a
- a. nail platelet.
- b. nail disorder.
- c. nail fungus.
- d. nail shape.

55. A nail fungus first appears as a
- a. black spot in the nail bed.
- b. red spot that spreads toward the free end of the nail.
- c. discoloration that spreads toward the cuticle.
- d. discoloration that gradually disappears.

56. A hypertrophied nail may be manicured as long as
- a. no infection is present.
- b. it does not cause pain.
- c. the client insists that you do so.
- d. you have special training.

The Skin and Its Disorders

57. Sweat glands in the body serve what function?
- a. to lubricate the skin
- b. to regulate the body's emotional response
- c. to stimulate sensory nerves and secrete hormones
- d. to regulate body temperature and secrete waste

58. Which of the following is NOT a function of the skin?
- a. protection
- b. sensation
- c. excretion
- d. digestion

59. A chronic inflammation of the sebaceous glands is referred to as
- a. acne.
- b. rosacea.
- c. steatosis.
- d. seborrhea.

60. The general term *dermatitis* is correctly used to refer to
- a. any inflammation of the skin.
- b. prickly heat.
- c. herpes simplex infection.
- d. only those skin conditions caused by allergies.

61. Your client asks you to remove a hair from a facial mole while you are arching her eyebrows. You should
a. go ahead and remove it.
b. do it, but wear sterile gloves.
c. refuse to remove it.
d. ask the salon owner for permission first.

62. A fiber that forms elastic tissue and gives the skin elasticity and flexibility is called
a. melanin.
b. collagen.
c. elastin.
d. dermis.

63. On what part of the body is the skin thickest?
a. buttocks
b. knee
c. palms and soles
d. nose

64. Subcutaneous tissue is located
a. above the epidermis.
b. above the cuticle.
c. below the adipose.
d. below the dermis.

Cells, Anatomy, and Physiology

65. The primary function of the skeletal system is to support the body and to
a. transport oxygen and food to body cells.
b. pump blood.
c. protect the internal organs.
d. digest food and excrete wastes.

66. The lower jawbone is known as the
a. maxilla.
b. mandible.
c. sphenoid bone.
d. occipital bone.

67. The cranial muscle that draws the front part of the scalp forward and wrinkles the forehead is the
a. frontalis.
b. epicranius.
c. corrugator.
d. orbicularis oculi.

68. Which sensory organ is surrounded by muscles that are not capable of movement?
a. eye
b. nose
c. tongue
d. ear

69. The vascular system consists of the
a. heart and blood vessels.
b. heart and lungs.
c. lungs and blood vessels.
d. liver and spleen.

70. Individual body cells receive food and oxygen through tiny blood vessels called
a. lymph ducts.
b. arteries.
c. capillaries.
d. veins.

71. The skin serves as an organ of the excretory system when a person
a. has goose pimples.
b. bleeds.
c. sweats.
d. faints.

72. Which statement about respiration is incorrect?
  a. The lungs are composed of thousands of tiny air sacs.
  b. With each breath, a person's lungs take in oxygen and eliminate carbon dioxide.
  c. A person can live many weeks without food, but only a few minutes without oxygen.
  d. A person's rate of breathing is always the same, regardless of activity level.

Electricity and Light Therapy

73. Name the two types of electric current.
  a. direct and indirect
  b. indirect and alternating
  c. alternating and direct
  d. direct and constant

74. The client should avoid contact with metal on chairs, stools, and jewelry during which electrotherapy treatment?
  a. faradic current
  b. sinusoidal current
  c. high-frequency current
  d. galvanic current

75. Which of the following is a facial treatment in which electrical equipment is used?
  a. electrotherapy
  b. electric treatment
  c. electrode massage
  d. electrolyte therapy

76. When using galvanic current,
  a. electrodes must be firmly wrapped with moistened cotton pledgets.
  b. the negative electrode must be placed on the area to be treated.
  c. both electrodes must be placed on the area to be treated.
  d. both electrodes must be placed on the back of the head.

77. The primary action of the Tesla (high-frequency) current is to
  a. contract muscles.
  b. relax muscles.
  c. produce heat.
  d. soften the tissues.

78. ________ is a unit that measures electrical pressure.
  a. An ohm
  b. An amp
  c. A volt
  d. A fuse

79. A substance that carries electricity is called a(n)
  a. circuit breaker.
  b. conductor.
  c. watt.
  d. amp.

80. A good conductor for applying electricity to the face and scalp is called a(n)
  a. conductor.
  b. volt.
  c. amp.
  d. electrode.

81. An electric current used to permanently destroy the root of the hair is called
  a. electrolysis.
  b. depilatory.
  c. photo-epilation.
  d. electronic tweezers.

82. The path of an electric current from the generating source through conductors and back to its original source is called a complete
  a. pathway.
  b. roundabout.
  c. circuit.
  d. conduction.

Chemistry

83. A neutral pH is
a. 4
b. 5
c. 6
d. 7

84. The main ingredient in shampoo is called a surfactant, which is also called
a. oil.
b. molecule.
c. detergent.
d. suspension.

85. Which chemical is the most strongly alkaline?
a. neutralizer
b. protein surfactant
c. water
d. sodium hydroxide

86. Which type of hair color uses pigment molecules of the greatest molecular weight?
a. temporary hair color
b. semipermanent hair color
c. tint
d. toner

87. Which of the following is an example of a water-in-oil emulsion?
a. permanent wave solution
b. cleansing cream
c. lightener
d. neutralizer

88. Many sculptured nail products are produced by using which of the following chemicals?
a. alum
b. boric acid
c. ethyl methacrylate
d. phenylenediamine

89. Elements are
a. substances that cannot be separated into simpler substances by ordinary means.
b. the same as atoms.
c. substances that are the structural units of atoms.
d. chemical combinations of two or more solids, liquids, or gases.

90. The ingredient in both styling gels and hairsprays that gives the hair body and texture is usually a type of
a. polymer.
b. kaolin.
c. acid.
d. lotion.

The Salon Business

91. Your local (town or city) laws usually dictate
a. income taxes.
b. renovations.
c. sales taxes.
d. health regulations.

92. Which level of government is usually responsible for setting income tax codes and rates?
a. local government only
b. local and state government
c. state government only
d. state and federal government

93. Of the major expenses involved in running a salon, the one that the owner can continually adjust at his or her own discretion, is
a. rent.
b. supplies.
c. salaries.
d. advertising.

94. A business plan is best described as a
a. balance sheet.
b. profit and loss statement.
c. map.
d. bank statement.

95. Which of the following is NOT included in a business plan?
a. a description of the business and services it will provide
b. a statement of the number of personnel to be hired
c. how the owner will use his or her profits from the business to purchase a swimming pool
d. an operations plan that includes price structure and expenses

96. Keeping careful inventory records of retail supplies helps to determine
a. when it is time to reorder.
b. what merchandise you should advertise.
c. how much your supplies cost.
d. each item's shelf life.

97. What can be used as a guideline for knowing how many employees to hire for your salon?
a. The number of clients will determine the number of salon employees.
b. The size of your salon will determine the size of your staff.
c. The number of retail lines offered will determine the number of salon employees.
d. The size of your parking facility will determine the size of your staff.

98. Which of the following is a sign of a poor and ineffective manager?
a. being honest with employees
b. acting as a mentor to staff
c. hiding information from staff
d. following the same rules as other employees

99. The correct way to answer the telephone in a salon is to say,
a. "Hi."
b. "What do you want?"
c. "This is Royal Salon, a full-service salon featuring European-style nail wrapping. Our business hours are 10 A.M. to 8 P.M., Monday through Saturday. Would you like to schedule an appointment?"
d. "Good morning, Royal Salon, Cindy speaking. How can I help you?"

100. The most courteous, effective way to deal with client complaints about salon service is to
a. listen to the client's whole story and then suggest a solution.
b. tell the client that no one has ever had that problem before.
c. tell the client that he or she should use another salon in the future.
d. agree with everything the client says at all times.

101. In trying to sell products to a client, your first consideration should always be
a. the client's best interest.
b. the salon's profit.
c. your commission.
d. the time of day and day of the week.

102. A salon typically spends what percentage of its gross income on advertising?
a. 1%
b. 3%
c. 10%
d. 30%

Physical Services

Draping

103. When using a protective neck strip and a cape, you should always be sure that the cape
a. is fastened as tightly as possible.
b. is under the neck strip.
c. does not touch the client's skin.
d. is a becoming style and color.

104. The purpose of careful draping is to
a. show consideration for the client.
b. show off your professional skills.
c. avoid lawsuits.
d. maintain sanitation.

105. What should you use when draping a client for a shampoo?
a. towel, cape, and another towel
b. towel and cape only
c. neck strip and cape
d. neck strip, cape, and towel

106. When using only a neck strip and cape for draping,
a. secure the cape first, and place the neck strip over it.
b. make sure that both are applied very loosely.
c. ask the client to hold the neck strip in place during the entire combout.
d. secure the neck strip first and then fold it down over the edge of the cape.

107. To protect your clients' clothing during a chemical texture service, have them
a. wear old clothes.
b. wear their formal attire as normal.
c. change into a salon gown before starting the service.
d. come dressed in their pajamas.

108. Before a chemical texture service, you should have your client remove
a. his or her shoes.
b. his or her earrings.
c. his or her contact lenses.
d. his or her anklet.

Shampooing, Rinsing, and Conditioning

109. Which statement about hair brushing is correct?
a. Nylon-bristle brushes are recommended for hair brushing.
b. Natural-bristle brushes are recommended for hair styling.
c. You should not brush a client's hair if the scalp is irritated.
d. Brush each section of hair three times before going on to the next.

110. Which statement about the temperature of water for shampooing is correct?
a. Make the shampoo water as hot as the client can stand it.
b. You should monitor the water temperature continuously.
c. Most clients prefer very hot or very cold water.
d. The temperature doesn't matter, as long as you use plenty of water.

111. When shampooing the back of the head, which is the proper way to raise the client's head?
a. Ask the client to support his or her head on his or her arms.
b. Ask the client to turn around and face the basin.
c. Support the client's head in your left hand.
d. Ask another worker to support the head.

112. The first step in removing excess shampoo and lather, before rinsing the hair, is to
a. towel the hair.
b. soak the hair.
c. use a blow-dryer.
d. squeeze the hair.

113. During a shampoo, some suds get into the client's eye, and she complains of burning and pain. You should
a. have the client see a doctor immediately.
b. seat the client upright and have her rinse her eye with cold water.
c. continue with the shampoo and report the incident later.
d. ask the client if she has any allergies; if not, continue with the shampoo.

114. Protein is added to shampoo to
a. dry the hair.
b. raise the pH of the shampoo.
c. control dandruff.
d. condition the hair.

115. Which statement about medicated shampoos is incorrect?
a. They are generally used to control excessive dandruff.
b. They may affect the color of tinted or lightened hair.
c. They are generally prescribed by a physician.
d. They are less expensive than many non-medicated shampoos that work just as well.

116. Acid-balanced rinses are used to
a. work together with acid-balanced shampoos.
b. preserve the color of tinted hair.
c. add temporary highlights.
d. add moisture.

Manicuring and Pedicuring

117. Before each manicure, you should clean the top of the manicure table with
a. hot water.
b. soap and water.
c. disinfectant.
d. antiseptic.

118. If you accidentally cut your client's skin during a manicure, you should
a. apply an antiseptic or powder alum to the cut.
b. advise the client to wash his or her hands with soap and water.
c. apply an adhesive bandage and do not polish the nail on that finger.
d. file an incident report and offer to call a doctor.

119. If it is necessary to cut a client's cuticles to remove them, you should be careful to
a. remove a portion of epidermis as well.
b. cut extremely close to the epidermis.
c. remove the cuticle in a single piece.
d. use a straight razor with a dull edge.

120. If a hand massage is given as part of a manicure, it is done before
a. nail shaping.
b. soaking.
c. the base coat.
d. the top coat.

121. What should you remember when giving a leg massage?
a. Use firm pressure over the shinbone.
b. Massage the calf muscles with an upward movement.
c. End about halfway between the knee and the groin.
d. Massage both legs at once.

122. A client asks you to trim away a corn that is causing her discomfort. You should
a. refer her to a physician or podiatrist.
b. refer her to an orthopedic surgeon.
c. ask your supervisor for permission.
d. do as the client requests immediately.

Advanced Nail Techniques

123. Before applying the nail wrap, you should buff the natural oil off the existing nail surface to
a. make the wrap adhere better.
b. remove diseased tissue.
c. make the nail as short as possible.
d. cause the existing nail to fall off sooner.

124. Sculptured nails are also known as
a. wrapped nails.
b. built-on nails.
c. designer nails.
d. artificial nails.

125. Which of the following is a corrective treatment that protects a fragile or damaged nail?
a. nail tip
b. nail cap
c. nail wrap
d. built-on nail

126. Which statement about nail tipping is correct?
a. Nail tips are used to correct broken or cracked nails.
b. When affixing nail tips, apply adhesive to the underside of the natural nail.
c. Nail tips are removed by filing down to the natural nail.
d. The nail tip is sized and shaped to fit the free edge of the client's nail.

127. How far down should the nail tip cover?
a. one-quarter of the natural nail plate
b. one-half of the natural nail plate
c. two-thirds of the natural nail plate
d. one-third of the natural nail plate

128. Before applying the nail tip, you must first apply what to the nail?
a. antiseptic
b. primer
c. adhesive
d. bonding glue

129. Nail tips are removed by soaking the nails in
a. colored polish.
b. clear polish.
c. warm water.
d. acetone.

130. Another name for acrylic liquid is
- **a.** acrylic.
- **b.** polymer.
- **c.** primer.
- **d.** monomer.

131. What two products are combined to form a built-on nail?
- **a.** powder and polish
- **b.** polymer and acetone
- **c.** acrylic and polish
- **d.** polymer and monomer

132. The substance that improves adhesion and prepares the nail surface for bonding with the acrylic material is called a
- **a.** primer.
- **b.** adhesive.
- **c.** powder.
- **d.** spray.

Theory of Massage

133. A kneading movement used in massage is
- **a.** petrissage.
- **b.** friction.
- **c.** effleurage.
- **d.** percussion.

134. The most stimulating massage movement is
- **a.** petrissage.
- **b.** friction.
- **c.** effleurage.
- **d.** percussion.

135. Percussion movements to the face should consist of
- **a.** light finger taps.
- **b.** medium finger taps.
- **c.** light knuckle raps.
- **d.** medium knuckle raps.

136. A form that refers to shedding and peeling of the horny layer of the skin is called
- **a.** exfoliation.
- **b.** emollient.
- **c.** cleanser.
- **d.** freshener.

137. The three types of muscular tissue are
- **a.** origin, insertion, and belly.
- **b.** striated, nonstriated, and cardiac.
- **c.** anterior, posterior, and frontalis.
- **d.** supinator, pronator, and flexor.

Facials

138. After you analyze the client's skin, the first step in a facial is
- **a.** applying cleansing cream.
- **b.** removing makeup.
- **c.** steaming the client's face.
- **d.** applying massage cream.

139. When removing cleansing cream, you should start at the client's
- **a.** back.
- **b.** chest.
- **c.** neck.
- **d.** forehead.

140. You should press out blackheads on a client with oily skin immediately after
- **a.** cleansing the face.
- **b.** massaging the face.
- **c.** steaming the face.
- **d.** applying an astringent lotion.

141. The purpose of using infrared rays or electric current during a facial is to
- **a.** deep cleanse the skin.
- **b.** increase the cost to the client.
- **c.** use expensive equipment.
- **d.** help lotion penetrate the skin.

142. Which statement about the diet for a client with acne is correct?
a. Acne is caused by specific food allergies; the client should have allergy testing.
b. The client should consult with a doctor about an appropriate diet.
c. You can safely tell the client to eliminate all fats and salt from the diet.
d. The client should avoid chocolate, nuts, and red wine, and limit fluid intake.

143. A cosmetologist who specializes in skin care is called
a. a cosmetician.
b. an esthetician.
c. a makeup artist.
d. a colorist.

144. Which of the following is NOT a common reason that clients give for dissatisfaction with facials?
a. The cosmetologist does not present him- or herself professionally.
b. The cosmetologist does not treat the client respectfully.
c. The cosmetologist does not follow correct sanitary procedures.
d. The cosmetologist is extremely organized and has all materials on hand.

145. For which skin type are pack facials recommended?
a. dry skin
b. oily skin
c. all skin types
d. aging skin

146. What skin types are hydrating masks recommended for?
a. combination skin
b. oily skin
c. dry and mature skin
d. blemished skin

Facial Makeup

147. In general, eye shadow that is darker than the client's iris will make her eyes appear
a. darker.
b. lighter.
c. bluer.
d. greener.

148. Your client has a very round face. Where should you apply corrective makeup?
a. down the sides of the face
b. on the cheekbones
c. on the nose and chin
d. at the top and bottom of the face

149. Where should you use a darker shade of foundation to correct a broad nose?
a. on the sides of the nose
b. above the nose
c. below the nose
d. down the sides of the face

150. You can use makeup to make very round eyes look wider by
a. shading the inner corner most heavily.
b. extending the shadow in close to the nose.
c. using very light shadow under the brows and in the crease.
d. extending the shadow past the outer corner of the eye.

151. The most natural and attractive shape of the eyebrows is
- **a.** an arch that follows the curved shape of the eye socket.
- **b.** an arch just below the curve of the eye socket.
- **c.** a straight line that follows the top of the eye socket.
- **d.** a straight line just below the top of the eye socket.

152. It is necessary to do an allergy test before
- **a.** doing facial makeup.
- **b.** arching eyebrows.
- **c.** applying artificial eyelash strips.
- **d.** applying semipermanent individual eyelashes.

153. After they are used for facial makeup, all washable linens, such as towels and capes, should be placed
- **a.** on the floor for laundry collection.
- **b.** in a drawer for reuse.
- **c.** in a closed laundry receptacle.
- **d.** immediately in the washing machine.

Hair Removal

154. Which statement about use of hot wax to remove hair is correct?
- **a.** The wax is applied in the opposite direction of hair growth.
- **b.** It is safe if hot wax gets into the client's eyes.
- **c.** The wax is removed in the opposite direction of hair growth.
- **d.** The wax is removed slowly and gently.

155. A skin-sensitivity test is necessary before using
- **a.** a hot-wax depilatory.
- **b.** a cold-wax depilatory.
- **c.** electronic tweezers.
- **d.** a chemical depilatory.

156. Which of the following methods removes hair permanently?
- **a.** waxing
- **b.** lasering
- **c.** sugaring
- **d.** epilating

157. To perform laser hair removal, you need to have
- **a.** no special training.
- **b.** specialized training.
- **c.** an additional license.
- **d.** a certification.

158. The removal of hair by means of an electric current that destroys the root of the hair is called
- **a.** electrolysis.
- **b.** electrology.
- **c.** photo depilation.
- **d.** laser epilating.

159. Which of the following can perform electrolysis?
- **a.** a licensed electrician
- **b.** a licensed esthetician
- **c.** a licensed electrologist
- **d.** a licensed cosmetologist

160. When is waxing a method of permanent hair removal?
- **a.** when the hair is coarse
- **b.** never
- **c.** when the hair is fine
- **d.** always

Chemical Services

Permanent Waving

161. Porosity refers to the hair's ability to
a. retain its curl.
b. hold a shape.
c. resist moisture.
d. absorb liquid.

162. The processing time used for the waving lotion depends on the hair's
a. porosity and texture.
b. texture and elasticity.
c. elasticity and density.
d. density and length.

163. To perm hair longer than six inches, you should use
a. an alkaline-based waving lotion.
b. an extra-long waving time.
c. small partings and a piggyback wrap.
d. small partings and a bricklay wrap.

164. In permanent waving, which wrapping technique is used to wrap the hair from the ends to the scalp?
a. a double-flat wrap
b. a croquignole perm wrap
c. a bookend wrap
d. a piggyback perm wrap

165. In permanent waving, what happens to the hair during the processing stage?
a. The hair is hardened.
b. The hair is lubricated.
c. Oil is added to the hair shaft.
d. The hair is softened.

166. In permanent waving, what happens to the hair during the neutralization stage?
a. The hair is softened.
b. The hair is hardened.
c. The hair is lubricated.
d. The hair is moistened.

167. You should apply waving lotion to the
a. top and bottom of each rod.
b. top of each rod only.
c. area between the rods.
d. client's top hairline and allow it to drip down slowly.

168. After rinsing the waving lotion from the hair, the next step is to
a. apply the neutralizer.
b. blot off excess water.
c. blow-dry the hair.
d. set and style the hair.

169. How can you determine if hair has been overprocessed in permanent waving?
a. Hair will have a strong cure pattern.
b. Hair is soft and supple.
c. Hair will be curlier at the scalp and straight on the ends.
d. Hair will be curlier at the ends and straighter at the scalp.

170. When you are doing a permanent wave, what type of hair color should NOT be permed over?
a. aniline-derivative tints
b. oxidative tints
c. temporary color
d. metallic salt tints

Hair Coloring

171. When used to describe a color, the word *tone* refers to
a. darkness.
b. porosity.
c. density.
d. warmth.

172. Which of the following is a secondary color?
a. pink
b. orange
c. teal
d. brown

173. Which of the following is NOT a tertiary color?
a. blue-green
b. red-violet
c. yellow
d. yellow-orange

174. What effect do complementary colors have on each other?
a. They develop each other.
b. They brighten each other.
c. They darken each other.
d. They neutralize each other.

175. Why is it important that you wear gloves when applying a temporary color rinse?
a. These products can stain the skin as well as the hair.
b. These products are highly toxic to the skin and eyes.
c. This avoids the spread of infection.
d. Most people are allergic to these products.

176. Because semipermanent hair-coloring products do not change the structure of the hair shaft, they are often used on clients who have
a. fine or damaged hair.
b. allergies to most hair-color products.
c. very dark hair.
d. coarse or very curly hair.

177. Permanent hair colors differ from temporary hair colors because they
a. both lighten and deposit color.
b. can only darken the hair.
c. cannot cause damage to fine hair.
d. can be used on previously tinted hair.

178. Hydrogen peroxide bleaches the color out of hair by
a. diluting the melanin globules and making them appear lighter.
b. allowing melanin to combine with oxygen and diffuse through the hair shaft.
c. coating the hair so that melanin cannot enter the cuticle layer.
d. acting as a solvent and diluting the solution of melanin and protein.

179. The advantage of single-process tints is that they can simultaneously
a. lighten the hair and add color.
b. darken and condition the hair.
c. cleanse and condition the hair.
d. lighten the hair and remove color.

180. To a colorist, the term *lift* refers to
a. color highlights.
b. natural sheen.
c. lightening action.
d. color matching.

181. Fading is a particular problem on hair that is tinted
a. red.
b. blonde.
c. dark brown.
d. black.

182. Your client's hair is tinted a medium red-brown, but she now requests a change to a lighter shade. It will be necessary for you to first
a. select a complementary tint.
b. add a filler tint.
c. recondition her hair before adding a semipermanent rinse.
d. remove the present tint.

183. Adding a lighter color in small, carefully selected areas is known as
a. backlighting.
b. tipping.
c. highlighting.
d. decolorizing.

184. A penetrating hair color is one that
a. washes out after approximately eight shampoos.
b. enters the cortex of the hair shaft.
c. is not mixed with a developer.
d. is not alkaline.

185. Melanin pigment is naturally present throughout the hair's
a. cuticle.
b. medulla.
c. cortex.
d. papilla.

186. When you add pigment to fine hair, the effect will be especially dark because
a. the melanin granules are grouped closely together.
b. there are more hairs per square inch.
c. fine hair contains more melanin than other types of hair.
d. fine hair contains more melanin granules than other types.

187. Before the client decides on a color service, it is important that you carefully explain
a. the process, cost, and upkeep involved.
b. the chemical process involved.
c. that you can guarantee that you will achieve a specific shade.
d. that hair coloring carries the risk for allergic reaction.

188. When should a patch test be given?
a. 24–48 seconds prior to application
b. 24–48 minutes prior to application
c. 24–48 hours prior to application
d. 24–48 days prior to application

189. You should choose a warm hair color for a client with which type of skin tone?
a. olive
b. red
c. neutral
d. golden

190. Green tones in a hair color usually result from
a. too much red in the mix.
b. reaction to a chemical, such as chlorine.
c. hair that is not sufficiently porous.
d. not enough orange in the mix.

191. Your client complains that her hair color is "too red." You determine that her hair is actually a level 7 orange. To neutralize the brassy tones, you should select a
a. level 7 green.
b. level 8 green.
c. level 7 blue.
d. level 8 blue.

192. Hydrogen peroxide should be stored in a
a. clear glass bottle in the refrigerator.
b. plastic container in a warm place.
c. opaque container in a cool, dark place.
d. clear glass container in direct sunlight.

193. Before the application of a toner, the hair must first be
a. decolorized.
b. prelightened.
c. pretinted.
d. single processed.

194. A very pale blonde color can be safely achieved by
a. one prolonged application of bleach.
b. using a combination of semipermanent and permanent hair colors.
c. lightening to pale yellow and then using a toner.
d. up to three applications of bleach.

195. In permanent hair color, the ingredient in professional tints is
a. aniline derivative.
b. metallic salt.
c. vegetable dye.
d. developer.

196. You remove a toner by
a. applying hydrogen peroxide to neutralize it.
b. shampooing twice.
c. brushing the hair vigorously.
d. wetting the hair and massaging it to a lather.

197. A color additive is
a. a hair-color product.
b. a semipermanent hair color.
c. a particular combination of dyes that make up a specific hair color.
d. a concentrated color used to intensify or tone down a hair color.

Chemical Hair Relaxing

198. During a relaxer test, the test strand of hair breaks. You should
a. refuse to treat the client's hair.
b. condition the client's hair.
c. do another test with a weaker solution.
d. recommend thermal hair relaxing to the client.

199. What should you do before chemically relaxing a client's hair with a no-base relaxer?
a. Protect the entire scalp with a petroleum cream.
b. Apply a protective cream to the hairline and ears.
c. Wet the client's hair.
d. Recommend thermal hair relaxing to the client.

200. When retouching a client's hair with a sodium hydroxide relaxer, you should
a. relax the entire head again.
b. relax only the curliest parts of the hair.
c. wait at least six months between treatments.
d. relax the new growth only.

201. A chemical hair relaxer that is formulated for fine, color-treated, or damaged hair would be labeled as what strength?
a. low strength
b. mild strength
c. regular strength
d. super strength

202. Relaxers with ammonium thioglycolate differ from relaxers with sodium hydroxide because thio relaxers are
a. milder.
b. quicker.
c. more dangerous.
d. hotter.

203. When giving a soft-curl perm, you should take a test curl frequently in order to ensure that the
a. hair is not becoming curlier.
b. hair is curling properly but not becoming damaged.
c. client's skin is not becoming irritated.
d. heat is not too great for the client to stand.

204. Which statement about chemically relaxed hair is correct?
a. You should not use a thio relaxer on hair previously treated with sodium hydroxide.
b. You should not use heat of any kind on chemically relaxed hair.
c. A protective base is always needed for a sodium hydroxide relaxer.
d. Never use sodium hydroxide on very fine hair.

Hair Design

Haircutting

205. In the five-section parting method, section 1 is located
a. from the forehead to the crown.
b. at the back of the head.
c. above the right ear.
d. above the left ear.

206. When holding haircutting scissors, you place your thumb
a. on the finger brace.
b. in the ring of the movable blade.
c. in the ring of the still blade.
d. on the pivot.

207. The terms *slithering* and *effiliating* refer to the process of
a. cutting tinted hair.
b. cutting very curly hair.
c. thinning the hair.
d. finger waving the hair.

208. In haircutting, what should you do after dividing the hair into sections?
a. Cut the hair in section 1.
b. Blunt cut sections 2 and 3.
c. Divide section 5 into two equal parts and blunt cut.
d. Decide on the length of the nape guideline hair.

209. To cut bangs, you should position yourself
a. in front of the client.
b. in back of the client.
c. on a low stool.
d. above the top of the client's head.

210. The guide for cutting each section of hair is the
a. nape hair.
b. height of the earlobe.
c. previously cut section.
d. crown hair.

211. A technique for creating fullness in a haircut by cutting the ends of the hair at a slight taper is called
a. razoring.
b. beveling.
c. texturing.
d. slithering.

212. In a blunt or one-length haircut, what degree of elevation is employed?
a. 90°
b. 45°
c. 30°
d. 0°

213. Which of the following is NOT a reason for using reference points in haircutting?
a. to ensure balance within the design
b. to allow for the re-creation of the same haircut again
c. to indicate where and when to change technique to compensate for irregularities in the head form
d. to determine the length the hair should be cut to

214. The area of the head between the apex and the back of the parietal ridge is called the
a. occipital bone.
b. crown.
c. top of the head.
d. sides of the head.

215. What do layers in a haircut create?
a. weight
b. texture
c. movement
d. tension

216. When cutting curly hair, you need to remember that it will
a. extend much more after it dries than straight hair.
b. change color much more after it dries than straight hair.
c. shrink much more after it dries than straight hair.
d. straighten much more after it dries than straight hair.

217. The clipper is used to
a. make the first guide cut.
b. finish off the crown hair.
c. trim the neck hair.
d. thin the hair.

Hairstyling

218. In finger waving, which statement about forming the first ridge is correct?
a. Emphasize the ridge by pushing it outward with your fingers.
b. The first ridge begins at the crown of the head.
c. The first ridge is formed by inserting the comb beneath your index finger and pulling forward.
d. With the teeth of the comb still inserted in the first ridge, you would next pull the hair away from the head.

219. The second ridge begins at the
  a. level of the earlobe.
  b. hairline level.
  c. nape of the neck.
  d. crown of the head.

220. Which statement about bases for pin curls is incorrect?
  a. The finished curl is affected by the shape of the base.
  b. Square-base curls should be staggered in a brick-laying format
  c. Triangular-base curls are used along the facial hairline.
  d. You subdivide sections of hair into bases for pin curls.

221. When you are shaping waved bangs with pin curls, what is the relationship between hair texture and number of pin curls?
  a. The finer the hair, the more pin curls.
  b. Normal hair should have exactly one pin curl per square inch.
  c. The coarser the hair, the more pin curls.
  d. There is no relationship.

222. After you remove the rollers and clips from a setting, the next step is to
  a. wet down the hair slightly.
  b. apply setting lotion.
  c. thoroughly brush the hair.
  d. back comb the hair.

223. Back combing is used to
  a. remove tangles from hair.
  b. add volume to a hairstyle.
  c. hide the roots of tinted hair.
  d. smooth out curl patterns.

224. A client with close-set eyes should have a hairstyle that is
  a. asymmetrical.
  b. swept back.
  c. wide at the bottom.
  d. wide at the top.

225. For a client with a long, thin neck, the hair should
  a. be upswept and full on top.
  b. fall in long, full waves.
  c. be asymmetrical.
  d. be very full around the face.

226. For a client with a protruding chin, you should create a hairstyle with fullness at the
  a. chin level.
  b. crown of the head.
  c. forehead.
  d. nape of the neck.

227. Practice with using thermal irons is intended to help you develop
  a. an impressive repertoire of moves.
  b. a smooth, rotating motion.
  c. strength in your grip.
  d. resistance to injury from heat.

228. After heating and rolling a full-base curl, place it
  a. forward and high on its base.
  b. in the center of its base.
  c. halfway off its base.
  d. completely off its base.

229. Which type of comb is NOT good for use with curling irons?
  a. metal or celluloid
  b. hard rubber
  c. heatproof plastic
  d. nonflammable material

230. When blow-drying hair, using a large-diameter brush results in
a. loose curls.
b. curly hair.
c. a long-lasting hairstyle.
d. a layered hairstyle.

231. When you are styling a client's hair with an air waver, it is most important to
a. follow the hair's natural waves.
b. have the hair completely dry first.
c. use a large-diameter brush.
d. cut the hair with blunt ends.

232. When you are making sure that a blown-dry hairstyle holds in place, it is most important to
a. cut the hair with blunt ends.
b. get the hair and scalp completely dry.
c. use the largest brush available.
d. use the hottest drying temperature the client can stand.

Thermal Hair Straightening

233. The rule for deciding on the size of the subsections to use when pressing hair is
a. the finer the hair, the larger the sections.
b. the finer the hair, the smaller the sections.
c. the curlier the hair, the larger the sections.
d. the curlier the hair, the smaller the sections.

234. You should control the heat carefully when pressing lightened or tinted hair because it is more likely to
a. frizz.
b. curl up.
c. discolor.
d. coarsen.

235. Very short hair presents particular problems in pressing because of the possibility that the
a. iron will burn the client.
b. hair will frizz or curl.
c. hair will fall out at the roots.
d. iron will not be hot enough.

236. How much curl does a hard press remove?
a. 40–50%
b. 60–74%
c. 75%
d. 100%

237. In the event of a scalp burn, you should immediately
a. reshampoo the client's hair.
b. apply 1% gentian violet jelly.
c. apply cotton balls dipped in ice water.
d. wet the area that has been burned with cold water and then apply a light dusting of talcum powder to absorb the heat.

Braiding and Braid Extensions

238. When you are braiding or weaving hair, it is best if the hair is
a. dry.
b. semidry.
c. semiwet.
d. wet.

239. A three-strand braid that employs the underhand technique, in which strands of hair are woven under the center strand, is called
a. an invisible braid.
b. an indivisible braid.
c. a visible braid.
d. a visual braid.

240. A man or a woman who wears narrow rows of visible braids that lie close to the scalp is wearing what type of braid?
a. visible
b. cornrow
c. underhand
d. invisible

241. Natural textured hair that is intertwined and meshed together to form a single or separate network of hair describes
a. hair locking.
b. hair stepping.
c. hair meshing.
d. hair winding.

242. If a bulb can be felt at the end of each lock, the hair begins to regain length and the locks are closed at the ends, dense and dull, not reflecting any light, what stage of maturation is the lock in?
a. prelock stage
b. sprouting stage
c. growing stage
d. maturation stage

243. To remove bonded wefts from the hair, you must soak them in
a. acetone.
b. warm water.
c. oil.
d. cool water.

244. What method of attachment is best for clients with fine, limp hair?
a. sew-and-cut method
b. bonding method
c. track-and-sew method
d. fusion method

245. What aspect of the track determines how the hair will fall?
a. reference
b. angle
c. length
d. cut

Wigs and Hair Enhancements

246. When ordering a wig for a client, you should specify the measurements, hair color, type of hair, length of hair, and
a. finished style.
b. hair parting and pattern.
c. client's eye color.
d. client's skin color.

247. You can stretch a wig that is too small by
a. wetting it, pinning it to a larger size block, and putting it under a hot dryer.
b. cutting it apart and resewing it.
c. wetting it, pinning it to a larger size block, and letting it dry naturally.
d. wetting it and letting it dry on the client's head.

248. When you cut and shape a wig, the best way to ensure that the style will suit the client's features is to
a. use a picture of the client as a guide.
b. cut it while it is on the client.
c. cut it to the client's directions.
d. use a picture of a model the client thinks is attractive.

249. Which statement about cutting a synthetic wig is correct?
a. Cut the wig while dry, using scissors and thinning shears.
b. Cut the wig while dry, using a razor.
c. Cut the wig while wet, using scissors and thinning shears.
d. Cut the wig while wet, using a razor.

250. When combing out a newly set wig, use a
a. narrow-tooth comb.
b. wide-tooth comb.
c. natural bristle brush.
d. wire bristle brush.

Answers

Scientific Concepts

Nutrition/Ergonomics

1. a. Good posture means standing with the back straight, head up, holding shoulders level, and no slouching.

2. b. Rest your body weight on the full length of your thighs while sitting to avoid constricting one specific area.

3. c. Ergonomics is a prevention of problems in our industry, such as musculoskeletal disorders. It is the ability to fit your work to your body and not your body to your work.

4. d. Musculoskeletal disorders (MSDs) include carpal tunnel syndrome, problems with the legs, feet, shoulders, wrists, and back, and tendonitis.

5. c. Gripping and/or squeezing implements too tightly can cause tendonitis and/or carpal tunnel syndrome.

Your Professional Image

6. b. Personal hygiene is very important in this industry because cosmetologists have very close contact with our clients. This includes changing clothes daily and washing hands after using the restroom and before and after clients.

7. c. Fast foods tend to be packed with sugar and fats, which are not healthy and can cause sluggishness and weight gain.

Infection Control and Federal Regulations

8. c. After each client, clean and clear the drain of hair and disinfect the bowl with a hospital-grade disinfectant.

9. b. Use 5% chlorine bleach to one gallon of water to disinfect a whirlpool pedicure chair.

10. d. The pedicure foot spa should be disinfected with a hospital-grade disinfectant, as it is not only a bactericide, but also a fungicide, virucide, and tuberculocide.

11. a. MSDS (Material Safety Data Sheets) are required by federal law. OSHA enforces these standards.

12. b. Only nonporous surfaces can be sterilized. To sterilize a porous surface such as a nail plate, for example, would destroy the nail plate.

Cells, Tissue, and Body Systems

13. d. Muscles should be massaged from insertion to origin, from the moveable part of a muscle (insertion) to the fixed part of a muscle (origin).

14. d. Otology is the scientific study of bones; OS is the technical term for bone.

15. a. The cell is the basic unit of all living matter; it is responsible for all processes.

16. d. The skin is the largest and most important organ of the body. Healthy skin is moist, soft, and flexible.

17. a. The average heart beats 72–80 times per minute in a normal resting state.

18. b. Physiology studies the function and activities performed by body structures.

19. a. The fifth cranial nerve, also known as the trifacial or trigiminal nerve, is the largest nerve. It is the chief sensory nerve of the face and the motor nerve of chewing.

20. c. Ten major systems compose the body: respiratory, reproductive, skeletal, nervous, muscular, integumentary, excretory, endocrine, digestive, and circulatory.

Bacteriology

21. c. The body's main defenses against infection are unbroken skin, white blood cells, body secretions, such as digestive juices, and antitoxins. Red blood cells have other functions within the body.

22. a. A carrier is someone who can transmit a disease to others without being sick him- or herself.

23. a. Ringworm is a fungal infection of the skin.

24. a. Using unsanitary implements can spread HIV. HIV can be spread only by the sharing of blood or other body fluids. For example, if you accidentally cut a person who has HIV and get blood on your scissors, the virus could be spread to another person unless the scissors are properly sanitized.

25. a. The most common pus-forming bacteria are staphylococci.

26. c. Cosmetologists should NOT treat skin diseases; instead, you should refer the client to a physician.

27. a. Nonpathogenic organisms are helpful and perform many useful functions, such as decomposing garbage.

28. d. Spirilla bacteria are shaped like corkscrews.

29. b. Cocci bacteria move through the air.

Decontamination and Infection Control

30. a. Disinfectants are used to kill microorganisms on nonliving surfaces only. They should never be used on human skin, hair, or nails.

31. b. Because disinfectants are such strong chemicals, you should always follow the manufacturers' directions when using them.

32. b. Always clean instruments thoroughly before placing them in disinfectant solution.

33. a. Quat is an effective and fast-acting disinfectant; *quat* is short for quaternary ammonium compound.

34. a. Always wear rubber gloves and goggles when handling powerful chemicals such as disinfectants in order to protect your hands and eyes.

35. c. Sanitation means keeping every item and surface in the salon clean and properly disinfected.

36. d. It is important to use the proper procedure when disinfecting a countertop. The incomplete procedures listed in the other answer choices are likely to leave potentially harmful materials on the countertop surface.

37. d. Ethyl alcohol must be used in a solution no weaker than 70% to be an effective disinfectant.

38. c. The solution used in a wet sanitizer should be changed every day.

Properties of the Hair and Scalp

39. c. The health of a person's hair is most influenced by the person's physical and emotional health.

40. a. A cowlick is a tuft of hair that stands straight up.

41. a. The cuticle is the outermost protective layer of the hair shaft.

42. c. The purpose of scalp manipulation (scalp massage) is to relax the client and to stimulate blood circulation in the scalp.

43. a. Oil treatments are beneficial for split ends. The other treatments mentioned would not help and might aggravate the problem.

44. d. A boil, or furuncle, is an acute, painful infection of a hair follicle.

45. b. Clients with head lice should never be treated in the salon, since head lice spread so easily. The other choices are correct statements about head lice.

46. d. The bulb of the hair fits around and over the papilla at the base of the hair shaft.

47. a. The shape and direction of the follicle determines the direction of hair growth.

48. c. The average person sheds approximately 35–40 hairs per day.

49. b. The three hair shapes are round, almost flat, and oval.

The Nail and Its Disorders

50. b. A normal, healthy nail grows forward, starting at the matrix and extending over the tip of the finger.

51. a. Younger people's nails grow more quickly than those of older people. The other statements are incorrect.

52. b. A nail that is lost because of disease will probably grow back distorted.

53. c. If a client is accidentally cut during a manicure, apply antiseptic and a sterile bandage to help prevent infection. The other answer choices are overreactions to a minor injury.

54. b. A nail disorder is a condition caused by injury to the nail or some disease or imbalance in the body.

55. c. A fungal infection in the nail most commonly appears as a discoloration that spreads toward the cuticle.

56. a. Manicure a hypertrophied nail as long as no infection is present. If an infection is present, you should refer the client to a physician.

The Skin and Its Disorders

57. d. The sweat glands regulate body temperature (primarily by helping to cool the body) and secrete waste products.

58. d. The main functions of the skin include protection, sensation, heat regulation, excretion, and secretion of sebum. Digestion is a function of the digestive system.

59. a. Acne is a chronic inflammation of the sebaceous glands and can occur anywhere on the body.

60. a. Dermatitis refers to any inflammation of the skin, no matter what the cause.

61. c. You should not remove hair from a mole.

62. c. Elastin is the fiber similar to collagen that forms elastic tissue and gives the skin the ability to stretch and contact to regain its shape.

63. c. The skin is the thickest on the palms of the hands and soles of the feet.

64. d. Subcutaneous tissue is located below the dermis. (Note: The prefix *sub*-means *below*.)

Cells, Anatomy, and Physiology

65. c. The skeleton supports and protects the internal organs. Specialized cells within the long bones also produce blood cells.

66. b. The lower jawbone is called the mandible.

67. a. The frontalis muscle controls the movement of the forehead.

68. d. The muscles surrounding the ear have almost no function.

69. a. The vascular system, which circulates blood throughout the body, consists of the heart and blood vessels.

70. c. The capillaries nourish individual body cells.

71. c. The skin's function as an excretory organ is to perspire, which rids the body of waste products.

72. d. A person's rate of breathing, rather than staying the same all the time, increases with increased activity.

Electricity and Light Therapy

73. c. The two types of electric current are direct current, which is a constant, even-flowing current that travels in one direction only and produces a chemical reaction, and alternating current, which is a rapid and interrupted current, flowing first in one direction and then in the opposite direction.

74. c. Whether you are using direct or indirect application of high-frequency current, a burn can occur.

75. a. Electrotherapy is a facial performed with electric facial machines to enhance the treatment.

76. a. When you use galvanic current, electrodes must be firmly wrapped with moistened pledgets, which are usually saturated with saltwater.

77. c. The Tesla current works by producing heat—is thermal and also germicidal.

78. c. Volts measure electrical pressure.

79. b. A conductor is a substance that carries or conducts electricity. Most metals are conductors.

80. d. Electrodes are usually made of glass and are applied directly to the skin and scalp during electrotherapy.

81. a. A fine-needle electrode is inserted into the follicle to destroy the root of the hair during electrolysis. Electrolysis must be performed by a licensed electrologist.

82. c. A complete circuit is the path of an electric current from the generating source through conductors and back to its original source.

Chemistry

83. d. A neutral pH reading—that is, an indication that a substance is neither acid nor alkaline—is 7.

84. c. Surfactants, also called detergents, cleanse.

85. d. Sodium hydroxide, which has a pH of 13, is strongly alkaline. It is a caustic chemical that must be handled with extreme caution.

86. a. Because of the large molecular weight of the pigment molecules, temporary hair colors cannot enter into the hair shaft, but rather remain on the surface.

87. b. Cleansing cream is a water-in-oil emulsion. The other choices are examples of oil-in-water solutions.

88. c. Ethyl methacrylate is a chemical compound used in many sculptured nails.

89. a. An element cannot be separated into a simpler substance by ordinary chemical means.

90. a. Polymers are chemicals that form long chains and thus coat the hair shafts and hold them in place.

The Salon Business

91. b. Permission to renovate a property is usually obtained from the local (town or city) government.

92. d. In most states, both the state and federal governments levy income taxes.

93. d. The business owner usually has the most control over advertising costs, which the owner can increase or decrease whenever he or she wants. Rent, supplies, and salaries are costs over which the owner has less control.

94. c. A business plan is most like a map in that it lays out all of the options you might take and helps you to chart the best route to your final goals.

95. c. The business plan includes every aspect of the business, but not how individuals will use the profits of their business, unless it is to be reinvested in the business.

96. a. Careful inventory records will help you reorder in time so you do not miss potential sales.

97. b. The size of your salon will determine the number of staffers you will need to hire to achieve maximum efficiency and productivity of the salon space.

98. c. Poor or ineffective managers are reluctant to share information with staff because they are afraid of losing power.

99. d. Be courteous, identify yourself, and ask what you can do for the client. On the other hand, don't go overboard with a long greeting; this may make the client impatient.

100. a. Always listen courteously to everything the client has to say before suggesting a solution.

101. a. Always consider the client's best interest. Providing good service will increase business in the long run.

102. b. A salon typically spends about 3% of its gross income on advertising.

Physical Services

Draping

103. c. Make sure that the cape does not touch the client's skin, where it can cause discomfort to the client.

104. a. Careful draping is important because it shows consideration for the client's comfort.

105. a. Wrap a towel over the client's shoulders, then the cape, and then another towel.

106. d. The neck strip should prevent any part of the cape from touching the client's skin.

107. c. To protect your client's clothing, have the client change into a gown and use a waterproof shampoo cape before beginning the service.

108. b. Have the client remove earrings, necklaces, and any other jewelry or adornment around the face, neck, and head.

Shampooing, Rinsing, and Conditioning

109. c. Never brush a client's hair if the scalp is irritated.

110. b. Monitor the water temperature continuously while shampooing to make sure it doesn't get uncomfortably hot or cold.

111. c. Support the client's head in your left hand while you manipulate the scalp with your right.

112. d. Squeeze the hair to remove excess lather before rinsing.

113. b. Have the client rinse the shampoo from her eye immediately to avoid additional irritation.

114. d. Protein is a conditioning agent.

115. d. Medicated shampoos are more expensive than other shampoos, but they are effective when prescribed by a physician to treat specific scalp conditions, such as problem dandruff.

116. b. Acid-balanced rinses are used to preserve the color of tinted hair and keep it from fading.

Manicuring and Pedicuring

117. c. Clean the manicure table with a disinfectant before each manicure in order to kill any potentially harmful bacteria.

118. a. If you accidentally cut your client's skin during a manicure, apply an antiseptic to prevent infection. Powered alum can be used to stop bleeding as it clots the blood over the cut.

119. c. Always remove the cuticle as a single piece.

120. c. The hand massage is done after the nail preparation and before applying nail polish.

121. b. Massage the calf muscles, moving toward the heart. You should not massage the shinbone or above the knee.

122. a. Do not treat corns, calluses, or ingrown toenails—this is a job for a physician, not a cosmetologist.

Advanced Nail Techniques

123. a. Using a fine grit file to remove natural oil from the nail plate and then applying a nail antiseptic to dehydrate the nail plate will allow the nail wrap to adhere better.

124. b. Sculptured nails are also known as built-on nails, since the nail extension is built on an existing foundation.

125. c. A nail wrap is a material placed over a natural nail or a tip that protects a nail that is brittle, fragile, or damaged from breakage. The wrap can be silk, linen, fiberglass, paper, or nylon.

126. d. Select a nail tip that fits the tip of the client's nail, and shape as needed.

127. b. A nail tip should never cover more than one-half of the natural nail plate.

128. a. Nail antiseptic must be applied to the natural nail before applying the nail tip to remove the remaining natural oil and to dehydrate the nail for better adhesion.

129. d. To remove nail tips, first remove any polish and place the client's fingertips in a bowl with enough acetone to cover the nails and soak them for the amount of time recommended by the manufacturer, and then use a fresh orangewood stick or a metal pusher to slide off the softened tips.

130. d. Monomer, also called liquid, is made up of many small molecules.

131. d. When combined on a brush, polymer (powder) and monomer (liquid) form a soft mound and can be placed on the nail form to build a nail enhancement.

132. a. A primer is a substance that improves adhesion, or attachment, and prepares the nail surface for bonding with the acrylic material.

Theory of Massage

133. a. Petrissage is a kneading movement.

134. d. Percussion, which consists of tapping or slapping movements, is the most stimulating type of massage.

135. a. Use light finger taps only to the face to avoid causing discomfort to the client and damaging sensitive tissues.

136. a. Exfoliation refers to shedding and peeling of the horny (outer) layer of the skin by an exfoliant ingredient, such as in an enzyme peel.

137. b. The three types of muscular tissue are striated (also called skeletal or voluntary muscles), nonstriated (also called involuntary, visceral, or smooth muscles), and cardiac (the heart).

Facials

138. a. Deep cleansing, which begins with the application of cleansing cream, is the first major step in a facial.

139. d. When removing cleansing cream, start at the forehead.

140. c. Remove blackheads with gentle pressure immediately after steaming the face, when the pores are open.

141. d. Heat and electric current stimulate the skin and help lotions and creams better penetrate.

142. b. Have the client consult with a physician about an appropriate diet.

143. b. An esthetician specializes in skin care.

144. d. The cosmetologist should be organized and have all materials readily available; the other choices are things the cosmetologist should not do.

145. c. Pack facials are recommended for all skin types and are usually applied directly to the skin.

146. c. Hydrating masks are recommended for dry and mature skin or skin that appears lifeless and dull. Gauze is often used to aid in holding the mask preparation on the face.

Facial Makeup

147. b. A darker eye shadow will generally make the eyes appear to be lighter.

148. a. Apply corrective makeup down the sides of the face for a client with a round face.

149. a. Blending a darker shade of foundation down the sides of the nose will minimize its width.

150. d. Extending the shadow out past the outer corner of the eye will make the eyes look wider.

151. a. Shape the eyebrow so that the curve follows the top of the eye socket.

152. d. An allergy test is necessary because of the adhesive used in semipermanent eyelashes.

153. c. For sanitary reasons, place used linens in a closed laundry receptacle immediately.

Hair Removal

154. c. Remove the wax quickly, in the opposite direction of hair growth.

155. d. A skin test is necessary before using a chemical depilatory.

156. b. Laser hair removal is a permanent form of hair removal.

157. b. In certain states and provinces, cosmetologists or estheticians are allowed to perform laser hair removal. This method requires specialized training, most commonly offered by laser equipment manufacturers.

158. a. The removal of hair by means of an electric current that destroys the root of the hair is called electrolysis.

159. c. Only a licensed electrologist may perform electrolysis.

160. b. Electrolysis, photo-epilation, and laser hair removal are the only forms of permanent hair removal.

Chemical Services

Permanent Waving

161. d. Porosity refers to the ability to absorb liquid.

162. a. Processing time depends on the hair's porosity and texture.

163. c. To perm hair longer than six inches, use small partings and the piggyback wrap or double tool technique because two tools are used on the subsection or strand of hair. The top half of the strand is rolled with one tool and the second half of the strand is rolled with the second tool.

164. b. Croquignole perm wrapping is wrapping the strand from the ends of the hair to the scalp. This produces a lighter cure on the ends and larger cure at the scalp due to the hair overlapping in layers when it is rolled on the tool. This is the most common type of perm.

165. d. The hair is softened during the processing stage; the perm wave solutions open the cuticle layer and allow the solution to penetrate into the cortex layer of the hair, which breaks the disulfide bonds to reshape hair around the rods to form a new cure pattern.

166. b. The hair is hardened during the neutralizing stage of perm waving. The processing is stopped and the disulfide bonds are rebuilt, which rehardens the hair to take on the new curl formation of the rod.

167. a. Apply waving lotion to the top and underside of each wound rod.

168. b. After rinsing, the next step is to blot excess water before applying neutralizer.

169. c. Overprocessed hair will be curlier at the scalp and straight on the ends or may even be completely straight. Too many disulfide bonds have been broken and will render too weak to hold curl and may appear frizzy.

170. d. Metallic salt tints are hair colors sold for home use and are not compatible with permanent waves. They coat the hair and perming can cause discoloration, uneven cure, and breakage of hair.

Hair Coloring

171. d. The term *tone* refers to the warmth or coolness of a color.

172. b. A secondary color is a color obtained by mixing equal parts of two primary colors. The secondary colors are green, orange, and violet.

173. c. A tertiary color is an intermediate color achieved by mixing a secondary color and its neighboring primary color on the color wheel in equal amounts. The tertiary colors include blue-green, blue-violet, red-violet, red-orange, yellow-orange, and yellow-green.

174. d. Because they are opposite on the color wheel, complementary colors neutralize each other.

175. a. Temporary rinses can stain the skin as well as the hair.

176. a. Semipermanent hair-coloring products are often used on clients with very fine or previously damaged hair.

177. a. Because permanent products both lighten and apply color, a wide range of effects are possible with these products.

178. b. Hydrogen peroxide is an oxidizer, a substance that allows oxygen to combine with another substance.

179. a. Single-process tints both lighten and add color in one step.

180. c. The term *lift* refers to a product's lightening action, that is, its ability to remove the natural hair color.

181. a. Fading is a particular problem with red tints.

182. d. It is necessary to remove the present, darker tint before adding a lighter one.

183. c. Adding color in selected areas is highlighting.

184. b. A penetrating color is one that enters the cortex of the hair shaft.

185. c. Melanin pigment is scattered throughout the cortex of each hair.

186. a. In fine hair, the melanin granules are grouped more closely together, so the effect is a darker color.

187. a. Make sure that the client understands all these factors, presented in a positive light, before making a decision.

188. c. The patch test must be given 24 to 48 hours prior to application, you must use the exact same type of color as will be used for the hair-color service, and the tint should remain undisturbed on the test site for 24 hours.

189. d. Warm hair colors are recommended for clients with golden skin tones.

190. b. Greenish tones most often result from reaction to a chemical in the environment, such as chlorine in a swimming pool.

191. d. Neutralize an unwanted color with a complementary color that is a shade darker; in this case, level 8 blue will neutralize a level 7 orange.

192. c. Both heat and light cause hydrogen peroxide to break down.

193. b. Before application of a toner, hair must be prelightened using a bleach to achieve a pale blonde color, and then toner should be applied. This is called a two-process, or double-process, application; as the toner is a pastel shade of a tint, the hair has to be prelightened first.

194. c. Lightening to pale yellow and then using a toner is the safe way to achieve a very light blonde color.

195. a. Aniline derivative is the ingredient in all professional tints and toners and requires a 24- to 48-hour patch test. It renders hair acceptable for other professional services such as permanent waves and relaxes.

196. d. Remove the toner by wetting the hair and massaging it until it lathers.

197. d. This is the correct definition of a color additive, which is also called a color concentrate.

Chemical Hair Relaxing

198. c. Part of the point of doing a test strand is to see how the client's hair will tolerate the treatment. If the test strand breaks, do another test using a milder solution.

199. b. When using a no-base product, apply a protective cream to the client's hairline and ears before applying the relaxer.

200. d. Relax only the new growth during a retouch.

201. b. A mild chemical hair relaxer is one that is formulated for fine, color-treated, or damaged hair and would be labeled in such a way as to avoid confusion over what strength it is.

202. a. Thio relaxers are milder and may thus be used on hair that is damaged, finer, or less curly.

203. b. Take frequent test curls to ensure that the curls are forming properly but the hair is not being damaged.

204. c. A protective base is always used with a sodium hydroxide relaxer.

Hair Design

Haircutting

205. a. Section 1 begins at the front hairline and extends to the top of the head.

206. b. The thumb is inserted into the ring of the movable blade.

207. c. *Slithering* and *effiliating* both refer to thinning the hair.

208. d. After sectioning, decide on the length of the nape guideline hair, and cut.

209. a. Stand in front of the client in order to cut bangs straight.

210. c. As you cut each section, use the previously cut section as a guide.

211. b. Beveling is the technique used for creating fullness in a haircut by cutting the ends of the hair at a slight taper. It is most often used with blunt cuts.

212. d. A blunt cut has no layers and therefore employs no elevation.

213. d. The length of the haircut is determined by the desired finished style.

214. b. The crown is the area between the apex and the back of the parietal ridge. It is important to identify any hair growth patterns in this area that may affect your finished cut.

215. c. A layered haircut is a graduated effect achieved by cutting the hair with elevation or overdirection. Layers create movement and volume in the hair by releasing weight.

216. c. The most important thing to remember when cutting curly hair is that curly hair behaves differently from straight hair after it is cut—for example, it shrinks much more after it dries than straight hair.

217. c. Clippers are used to trim the client's neck hair.

Hairstyling

218. c. The correct procedure for forming the first ridge is to position the comb under your index finger and pull forward.

219. d. The first ridge begins at the hairline, and the second begins at the crown of the head.

220. a. The finished curl is not affected by the shape of the base. The other statements about pin curls are all correct.

221. a. Finer hair requires a larger number of pin curls.

222. c. Brushing is the next step after removing rollers and pins.

223. b. Back combing adds volume to a hairstyle.

224. d. For close-set eyes, create fullness at the top; the style should be fairly high with a side movement.

225. b. Long, full waves of hair will minimize a long, thin neck.

226. c. Balance a protruding chin by creating a hairstyle with fullness over the forehead.

227. b. Smooth rotating motions are essential to the correct use of the thermal iron.

228. b. A full-base curl should be placed firmly in the center of its base.

229. a. Do not use a metal or celluloid comb; a metal comb can burn the client, and a celluloid comb can catch on fire.

230. a. The larger diameter the brush, the looser the curls.

231. a. An air waver is most successful if you locate and follow the hair's natural waves.

232. b. A blown-dry style will not hold if both the hair and scalp are not completely dry at the end of styling.

Thermal Hair Straightening

233. a. The size of the subsections is determined by the hair's texture, not by how curly it is.

234. c. Tinted or lightened hair is more likely to discolor when pressed.

235. a. With very short hair, take particular care to avoid burning the client's skin.

236. d. A hard press is a technique that removes 100% of the curl by applying the pressing comb twice on each side of the hair.

237. b. In the event of an accidental scalp burn, immediately apply 1% gentian violet jelly.

Braiding and Braid Extensions

238. a. It is best to braid hair when it is dry because if the hair is braided wet, it shrinks and recoils as it dries and may create excess pulling and tension.

239. c. A visible braid is a three-strand braid that employs the underhand technique, in which strands of hair are woven under the center strand.

240. b. Cornrows, or canerows, are narrow rows of visible braids that lie close to the scalp, worn by men, women, and children, and can be braided on hair of various lengths and textures. These flat contoured styles can last several weeks when applied without extensions and up to two months when applied with extensions.

241. a. Hair locking, also called dreadlocks, is natural textured hair that is intertwined and meshed together to form a single or separate network of hair.

242. c. During the growing stage, the bulb can be felt at the end of each lock and the hair grows longer.

243. c. To remove bonded wefts, you must first dissolve the adhesive bond with oil or bond remover, then gently pull the weft from the hair.

244. d. Fusion is a good choice for clients with fine, limp hair because bonding and tracking create bulk at the base that is too bulky and obvious with fine hair.

245. b. The angle at which the track is attached to the supporting braid is what will determine how the hair will fall.

Wigs and Hair Enhancements

246. b. The manufacturer needs information not only about the measurements and hair color, type, and length, but also about the hair parting and pattern.

247. c. The correct procedure for stretching a wig that is too small is to wet it, pin it to a larger block, and let it dry naturally.

248. b. It is often advisable to cut a wig while the client is wearing it.

249. a. Cut synthetic wigs while dry, and do not use a razor.

250. b. Use a wide-tooth comb to avoid damaging the hair of the wig.

LESSON 5

COSMETOLOGY PRACTICE EXAM 2

LESSON SUMMARY

This is the second of four practice exams based on the core content of your cosmetology coursework. Having taken one exam and having reviewed the Cosmetology Refresher Course, you should feel more confident about your ability to pick the correct answers. As you take this test, remember that knowing what to expect helps you feel better prepared.

Like the first 100-question exam in this book, this test is similar to the official cosmetology certification exam that you will take. This time around, you know more about how the exam is put together because you have seen many sample multiple-choice questions and are perhaps beginning to notice patterns in the order of questions. For example, you see that questions in each content area are grouped together. This pattern will help you develop your own test-taking strategy.

If you're following the LearningExpress Test Preparation System, you have done some studying between the first exam and this one and have also practiced your test-taking skills in Lesson 4. This second exam will give you a chance to see how much you have improved.

As before, the answer sheet follows this page, and the test is followed by the answer key. Pay attention to the explanations in the answer key, especially for the questions you missed.

Practice Test 2

1. ⓐ ⓑ ⓒ ⓓ
2. ⓐ ⓑ ⓒ ⓓ
3. ⓐ ⓑ ⓒ ⓓ
4. ⓐ ⓑ ⓒ ⓓ
5. ⓐ ⓑ ⓒ ⓓ
6. ⓐ ⓑ ⓒ ⓓ
7. ⓐ ⓑ ⓒ ⓓ
8. ⓐ ⓑ ⓒ ⓓ
9. ⓐ ⓑ ⓒ ⓓ
10. ⓐ ⓑ ⓒ ⓓ
11. ⓐ ⓑ ⓒ ⓓ
12. ⓐ ⓑ ⓒ ⓓ
13. ⓐ ⓑ ⓒ ⓓ
14. ⓐ ⓑ ⓒ ⓓ
15. ⓐ ⓑ ⓒ ⓓ
16. ⓐ ⓑ ⓒ ⓓ
17. ⓐ ⓑ ⓒ ⓓ
18. ⓐ ⓑ ⓒ ⓓ
19. ⓐ ⓑ ⓒ ⓓ
20. ⓐ ⓑ ⓒ ⓓ
21. ⓐ ⓑ ⓒ ⓓ
22. ⓐ ⓑ ⓒ ⓓ
23. ⓐ ⓑ ⓒ ⓓ
24. ⓐ ⓑ ⓒ ⓓ
25. ⓐ ⓑ ⓒ ⓓ
26. ⓐ ⓑ ⓒ ⓓ
27. ⓐ ⓑ ⓒ ⓓ
28. ⓐ ⓑ ⓒ ⓓ
29. ⓐ ⓑ ⓒ ⓓ
30. ⓐ ⓑ ⓒ ⓓ
31. ⓐ ⓑ ⓒ ⓓ
32. ⓐ ⓑ ⓒ ⓓ
33. ⓐ ⓑ ⓒ ⓓ
34. ⓐ ⓑ ⓒ ⓓ
35. ⓐ ⓑ ⓒ ⓓ
36. ⓐ ⓑ ⓒ ⓓ
37. ⓐ ⓑ ⓒ ⓓ
38. ⓐ ⓑ ⓒ ⓓ
39. ⓐ ⓑ ⓒ ⓓ
40. ⓐ ⓑ ⓒ ⓓ
41. ⓐ ⓑ ⓒ ⓓ
42. ⓐ ⓑ ⓒ ⓓ
43. ⓐ ⓑ ⓒ ⓓ
44. ⓐ ⓑ ⓒ ⓓ
45. ⓐ ⓑ ⓒ ⓓ
46. ⓐ ⓑ ⓒ ⓓ
47. ⓐ ⓑ ⓒ ⓓ
48. ⓐ ⓑ ⓒ ⓓ
49. ⓐ ⓑ ⓒ ⓓ
50. ⓐ ⓑ ⓒ ⓓ
51. ⓐ ⓑ ⓒ ⓓ
52. ⓐ ⓑ ⓒ ⓓ
53. ⓐ ⓑ ⓒ ⓓ
54. ⓐ ⓑ ⓒ ⓓ
55. ⓐ ⓑ ⓒ ⓓ
56. ⓐ ⓑ ⓒ ⓓ
57. ⓐ ⓑ ⓒ ⓓ
58. ⓐ ⓑ ⓒ ⓓ
59. ⓐ ⓑ ⓒ ⓓ
60. ⓐ ⓑ ⓒ ⓓ
61. ⓐ ⓑ ⓒ ⓓ
62. ⓐ ⓑ ⓒ ⓓ
63. ⓐ ⓑ ⓒ ⓓ
64. ⓐ ⓑ ⓒ ⓓ
65. ⓐ ⓑ ⓒ ⓓ
66. ⓐ ⓑ ⓒ ⓓ
67. ⓐ ⓑ ⓒ ⓓ
68. ⓐ ⓑ ⓒ ⓓ
69. ⓐ ⓑ ⓒ ⓓ
70. ⓐ ⓑ ⓒ ⓓ
71. ⓐ ⓑ ⓒ ⓓ
72. ⓐ ⓑ ⓒ ⓓ
73. ⓐ ⓑ ⓒ ⓓ
74. ⓐ ⓑ ⓒ ⓓ
75. ⓐ ⓑ ⓒ ⓓ
76. ⓐ ⓑ ⓒ ⓓ
77. ⓐ ⓑ ⓒ ⓓ
78. ⓐ ⓑ ⓒ ⓓ
79. ⓐ ⓑ ⓒ ⓓ
80. ⓐ ⓑ ⓒ ⓓ
81. ⓐ ⓑ ⓒ ⓓ
82. ⓐ ⓑ ⓒ ⓓ
83. ⓐ ⓑ ⓒ ⓓ
84. ⓐ ⓑ ⓒ ⓓ
85. ⓐ ⓑ ⓒ ⓓ
86. ⓐ ⓑ ⓒ ⓓ
87. ⓐ ⓑ ⓒ ⓓ
88. ⓐ ⓑ ⓒ ⓓ
89. ⓐ ⓑ ⓒ ⓓ
90. ⓐ ⓑ ⓒ ⓓ
91. ⓐ ⓑ ⓒ ⓓ
92. ⓐ ⓑ ⓒ ⓓ
93. ⓐ ⓑ ⓒ ⓓ
94. ⓐ ⓑ ⓒ ⓓ
95. ⓐ ⓑ ⓒ ⓓ
96. ⓐ ⓑ ⓒ ⓓ
97. ⓐ ⓑ ⓒ ⓓ
98. ⓐ ⓑ ⓒ ⓓ
99. ⓐ ⓑ ⓒ ⓓ
100. ⓐ ⓑ ⓒ ⓓ

Practice Exam 2

1. The daily maintenance of personal cleanliness and healthfulness is known as
   a. personal hygiene.
   b. preventive health care.
   c. cosmetology.
   d. relaxation.

2. The most important thing to consider when selecting shoes to wear at work is
   a. comfort.
   b. color.
   c. style.
   d. quality of leather.

3. Who requires a manufacturer to provide cosmetologists with an MSDS?
   a. EPA
   b. state law
   c. federal law
   d. state board

4. Who enforces the safety and health standards in a school or salon?
   a. U.S. Department of Education
   b. OSHA
   c. EPA
   d. state and local government

5. Cosmetologists need to understand bacteriology in order to
   a. prevent the spread of disease.
   b. discuss biology with clients.
   c. avoid contracting food-borne illnesses.
   d. avoid spreading HIV in the salon.

6. Which microorganisms are unable to move on their own and are spread through the air?
   a. treponema
   b. microspira
   c. mycobacterium tuberculosis
   d. streptococci

7. In a salon, contagious disease may be spread through direct contact between people or through use of
   a. very hot or very cold water.
   b. unsanitary tools and supplies.
   c. infection-control procedures.
   d. nonpathogenic bacteria.

8. In an active or vegetative stage, bacteria
   a. grow and reproduce.
   b. are destroyed.
   c. remain dormant.
   d. dry up and float on dust particles.

9. What information does a Material Safety Data Sheet contain pertinent to the usage and storage of disinfectants?
   a. why it is necessary to use disinfectants
   b. how to market the product to your clients
   c. whether it is safe to use the product on skin
   d. the content, associated hazards, and storage requirements of the products

10. In a salon, commercial disinfectants are used to
    a. wash hands.
    b. launder gowns.
    c. sterilize instruments and tools.
    d. clean floors and countertops.

11. Which of the following refers to gray hair?
a. fragilitas crinium
b. tinea
c. pityriasis
d. canities

12. The hair root is located
a. above the skin's surface.
b. below the skin's surface.
c. on the outside of the hair shaft.
d. on the inside of the hair shaft.

13. Seen in cross section, wavy hair appears to be
a. round.
b. oval.
c. almost flat.
d. completely flat.

14. Cosmetologists use ___________ to describe the acidity or alkalinity of a product.
a. cosmetologist chemistry
b. the Richer scale
c. the pH scale
d. alkali

15. The purpose of a general scalp treatment is to
a. cure infectious skin conditions.
b. keep the scalp and hair healthy.
c. eliminate dandruff and itchy scalp.
d. prepare the client for electrolysis.

16. Your client has round, red patches on her scalp and brittle hair that is broken off at the base in many places. You should refer this client to a physician for treatment of
a. favus.
b. ringworm.
c. scabies.
d. head lice.

17. Which part of the nail structure contains actively growing tissue?
a. nail plate
b. matrix
c. nail root
d. free edge

18. You should NOT manicure a nail that shows signs of
a. atrophy.
b. pterygium.
c. white spots.
d. onychomycosis.

19. Corrugations and furrows in the nail can be caused by pregnancy, illness, or
a. injury.
b. heart disease.
c. infection.
d. nerves.

20. The human skin is thinnest over the
a. soles of the feet.
b. palms of the hands.
c. eyelids.
d. ears.

21. A mosquito bite is an example of which type of skin lesion?
a. cyst
b. macule
c. papule
d. weal

22. Your client has developed several persistent, moist lesions on her face and arms. You should suggest that the client
a. try lotions appropriate for oily skin.
b. try a glycolic peel.
c. see a doctor for diagnosis and treatment.
d. consult a cosmetology textbook.

23. Which group of bacteria contain parasites that cause disease when they invade plant or animal tissue?
a. nonpathogenic
b. muscle reducing
c. pathogenic
d. virus

24. What kind of muscle are the muscles in the arms and legs?
a. involuntary muscle
b. voluntary muscle
c. smooth muscle
d. cardiac muscle

25. The muscles located in the hand are the
a. trapezius and latissimus dorsi muscles.
b. abductors, adductors, and opponent muscles.
c. pectoralis major and minor and serratus anterior muscles.
d. biceps, triceps, and deltoid muscles.

26. The large blood vessel that supplies blood to the head, face, and neck is the
a. carotid artery.
b. jugular vein.
c. angular artery.
d. angular vein.

27. Which of the following is NOT a safe way to use electricity?
a. plugging only one appliance into each outlet
b. replacing blown-out fuses with fresh ones
c. checking electric cords regularly for fraying
d. handling electric equipment with wet hands

28. When using ultraviolet rays, the cosmetologist and the client should always wear
a. sunscreen.
b. safety glasses.
c. rubber gloves.
d. long sleeves.

29. A whitish discoloration of the nails, caused by injury to the base of the nail, is called
a. leukonychia.
b. melanonychia.
c. onychatrophia.
d. pterygium.

30. Humectants, which temporarily attract and hold moisture, are an important ingredient in
a. protein conditioners.
b. instant conditioners.
c. shampoos.
d. neutralizers.

31. The chemical reaction that occurs when hair is bleached lighter is the
a. formation of a melanin solution.
b. dilution of a melanin solution.
c. diaphoresis of melanin.
d. oxidation of melanin.

32. Moisturizing creams work by
a. creating a barrier that lets the skin's natural fluids accumulate.
b. forcing moisture to enter the skin through a chemical reaction.
c. bonding with the skin's natural oil and moisture.
d. stimulating the skin to produce additional moisture.

33. Brushing the hair prior to shampooing
 a. pulls the hair and makes it limp.
 b. affects the color of the hair.
 c. stimulates blood circulation and loosens dirt and debris.
 d. could cause damage to the hair shaft.

34. How should facial manipulations be applied?
 a. fast and lightly
 b. in a slow, rhythmic, even tempo
 c. in a brightly lit room
 d. in a fast, even tempo

35. Dry skin is caused by
 a. overactive sebaceous glands.
 b. underactive sebaceous glands.
 c. overactive thyroid gland.
 d. underactive thyroid gland.

36. The two most important principles behind a successful sale are to know your merchandise and to
 a. adapt your sales pitch to the client's needs.
 b. tell the client anything he or she wants to hear.
 c. always assume that the client knows nothing about the product.
 d. sell additional products.

37. You have just draped a client for haircutting. The reason that you remove the outer towel and replace it with a neck strip is to
 a. keep the client from becoming overheated.
 b. make the client look more attractive.
 c. protect the client's face and neck.
 d. allow the hair to fall to the floor.

38. Before applying chemicals to the hair, you should apply a cream around the client's hairline in order to
 a. avoid a lawsuit.
 b. test for allergic reaction.
 c. sell additional products.
 d. avoid skin irritation.

39. Soft water is preferable to hard water for shampooing because it
 a. holds its temperature better.
 b. works up a better lather.
 c. feels softer on the client's skin.
 d. does not contain minerals.

40. The purpose of hair brushing is to stimulate the scalp and to
 a. provide a substitute for a scalp massage.
 b. provide a substitute for a shampoo.
 c. loosen natural curls and change the hair's texture.
 d. remove dust, dirt, and hairspray buildup.

41. The professional cosmetologist's responsibility regarding shampoo products is to
 a. sell a large number of different products.
 b. select the right one for each client.
 c. have a complete understanding of shampoo chemistry.
 d. encourage the client to make his or her own choices.

42. How do you remove light-cured gel nails?
 a. Soak them in acetone.
 b. Buff them layer by layer.
 c. Pour adhesive over them.
 d. Apply acetone and put them under a UV light source.

43. Nail hardeners are applied just before the
a. cuticles are cut.
b. base coat is applied.
c. nail dryer is applied.
d. polish is applied.

44. What should you avoid when removing old nail polish?
a. chipping the polish
b. getting the nail wet
c. smearing polish onto the cuticles
d. using too much nail polish remover

45. The purpose of a hand massage is to
a. earn money for the salon.
b. make the client's hands relaxed and flexible.
c. make nail polish adhere better.
d. impress the client with your knowledge and skill.

46. A discoloration in the natural nail after sculptured nails are applied usually indicates that the
a. nail has developed a fungus infection.
b. sculptured nail is correctly bonded to the natural nail.
c. client needs a darker shade of polish.
d. natural nail has died.

47. Which of the following can a cosmetologist treat in a pedicure?
a. corns
b. athlete's foot
c. infected, ingrown nails
d. overgrown toenails

48. The correct direction in which to massage a muscle is from the
a. point of insertion to the point of origin.
b. middle to the point of insertion.
c. middle to the point of origin.
d. point of origin to the point of insertion.

49. You should avoid vigorous massage of joints if your client
a. is elderly.
b. is overweight.
c. has diabetes.
d. has arthritis.

50. The cosmetologist should be knowledgeable of skin diseases so as to
a. know when to advise a client to seek medical treatment.
b. know what lotions to apply.
c. prescribe the correct medication.
d. know what type of oil to use.

51. The primary purpose of steaming the face is to
a. open the pores.
b. tighten the muscles.
c. clean the skin.
d. eliminate wrinkles.

52. For a client with dry skin, you should avoid the use of
a. infrared rays.
b. galvanic current.
c. lotions containing alcohol.
d. facial masks or packs.

53. Gauze, or cheesecloth, is used to hold mask ingredients that
- a. would be messy if applied directly to the skin.
- b. are too acidic to come in direct contact with the skin.
- c. are very hot or cold.
- d. would be very expensive if used on their own.

54. Before applying facial makeup for a client, you should be sure that your hands are clean and that
- a. the client has signed a release form.
- b. all applicators are sanitized or new.
- c. you agree with the client's color choices.
- d. the client's hair-care procedures are completed.

55. Before applying cheek color, you should ask the client to
- a. frown.
- b. smile.
- c. laugh.
- d. suck in her cheeks.

56. Corrective makeup for a bulging forehead consists of applying
- a. darker foundation over the prominent area.
- b. lighter foundation within the prominent area.
- c. lighter foundation below the prominent area.
- d. darker foundation all around the prominent area.

57. Which should you avoid when cutting toenails during a pedicure?
- a. cutting toenails straight across
- b. cutting toenails too deeply into the corners
- c. using sanitized toenail clippers
- d. using a sanitized foot bath

58. Another name for dandruff is
- a. canities.
- b. pityriasis.
- c. dermatitis.
- d. psoriasis.

59. Another name for male pattern baldness is
- a. canities.
- b. alopecia.
- c. alopecia areata.
- d. androgenic alopecia.

60. In hair designing, unequal proportions are referred to as
- a. asymmetrical.
- b. emphasis.
- c. symmetrical.
- d. harmony.

61. There are seven facial shapes. Which one are you trying to create an illusion of?
- a. round
- b. oval
- c. oblong
- d. triangle

62. A curl that rests on base after winding will produce the greatest degree of
- a. fullness.
- b. tightness.
- c. smoothness.
- d. glossiness.

63. Which procedure should you use if a client wants both a perm and hair coloring?
a. Tint the hair first, then perm it later the same day.
b. Perm the hair first, then tint it one week later.
c. Apply both chemicals at the same time.
d. Perform either procedure first, but wait at least a day before doing the second.

64. At what temperature do alkaline waves process?
a. heated temperature
b. room temperature
c. freezing temperature
d. below zero temperature

65. When should a patch test be performed on a client to determine whether or not there is an allergy to an aniline-derivative tint?
a. immediately before the hair coloring is done
b. one hour before the hair coloring is done
c. 24–28 hours before the hair coloring is done
d. immediately after the hair coloring is done

66. Cool-toned colors are those in which
a. blue predominates.
b. red predominates.
c. yellow predominates.
d. no black is present.

67. Approximately how long do deposit-only hair-coloring products last?
a. one to two weeks
b. two to four weeks
c. four to six weeks
d. six to eight weeks

68. The correct procedure for applying lightener to the hair shaft is to begin
a. at the root and apply liberally down to the ends.
b. one-half inch from the scalp and work down to the ends.
c. in the middle and stop one-half inch from the ends and one-half inch from the scalp.
d. at the ends and work to within one inch of the scalp.

69. The oxidizing agent that, when mixed with an oxidative hair color, supplies the necessary oxygen gas to develop color molecules and create a change in hair color is called
a. formulator.
b. developer.
c. constructor.
d. regulator.

70. You are covering the gray hair in your client's salt-and-pepper hair. You should select a shade that is
a. darker than the natural dark hair.
b. the same as the natural shade.
c. lighter than the natural shade.
d. a blend of the natural shade and the gray tone.

71. The chemical process involving the diffusion of the natural color pigment or artificial color from the hair is called hair
a. coloring.
b. streaking.
c. glazing.
d. lightening.

72. The Level System is a way of analyzing the
a. tone of a hair color.
b. texture of the hair.
c. absence or presence of pigment in the hair.
d. lightness or darkness of a color.

73. The primary colors are
a. green, purple, and orange.
b. red, blue, and green.
c. red, brown, and yellow.
d. blue, red, and yellow.

74. Semipermanent hair colors are a good choice for a client who
a. wishes to go only one shade lighter.
b. has selected a difficult-to-achieve shade.
c. wants the color to last only until the next shampoo.
d. is just beginning to turn gray.

75. A lightener and ____________ would be used in a double-process application of hair color.
a. a toner or tint
b. a semipermanent hair color
c. a mousse
d. hydrogen peroxide

76. Which should NOT be done when draping a client for hair-color services?
a. Slide a towel down from the back of the client's head and place it lengthwise across the client's shoulders.
b. Cross the ends of the towel beneath the chin and place the cape over the towel.
c. Leave the cape open in the back for comfort.
d. Fold the towel over the top of the cape and secure it in front.

77. The purpose of the petroleum cream in base-formula hair relaxers is to
a. increase the speed of the reaction.
b. decrease the heat of the reaction.
c. protect the client's skin and scalp.
d. protect the cosmetologist's hands.

78. When applying relaxer to the client's hair, you would
a. massage it into the entire head with your palms and fingers.
b. apply it to the scalp first and stretch each strand out tight.
c. spread it out evenly over the top and bottom of each small strand.
d. brush it vigorously through each section of hair with a wire brush.

79. You should NOT give a soft-curl perm to a client whose hair has been
a. relaxed with sodium hydroxide.
b. bleached with peroxide.
c. tinted.
d. given a conditioning treatment.

80. A good hairstyle will accentuate the client's good features while it
a. costs a great deal of money.
b. changes the texture of the hair.
c. minimizes the negative ones.
d. takes a very short time.

81. For what reason would it be necessary to thin a client's hair?
a. to remove excess bulk
b. to make hair less curly
c. to make hair appear fuller
d. to improve the texture of hair

82. Which of these are two basic lines used in haircutting?
a. straight and round
b. straight and curve
c. straight and diagonal
d. diagonal and curved

83. What type of lines are used to create one-length and low-elevation haircuts because they build weight?
a. diagonal
b. horizontal
c. curved
d. vertical

84. Before cutting section 2 at the crown of the head, you would divide it
a. into three vertical strips.
b. into pie-shaped wedges.
c. horizontally.
d. into four quarters.

85. Which of the following is NOT a type of stitch used to sew the extension to the track?
a. lock stitch
b. double-lock stitch
c. bonding stitch
d. overcast stitch

86. When should finger waves NOT be combed out?
a. after using waving lotion
b. after the hairnet is put on
c. before the hair is completely dry
d. before the left side is waved

87. The curl is given its direction and mobility from which part of the pin curl?
a. base
b. stem
c. circle
d. clip

88. You can create a longer-lasting curl by
a. stretching the hair strand and applying tension.
b. using very small amounts of hair in each strand.
c. making the pin curl very wide.
d. rotating the pin curl counterclockwise.

89. Which structure of the hair contains the blood and nerves needed for hair growth?
a. papilla
b. follicle
c. cuticle
d. bulb

90. What should be your goal when designing a hairstyle for a client with a round face?
a. to add the illusion of height to the face
b. to create the illusion of length to the hair
c. to create the illusion of width to the forehead
d. to reduce the width across the cheekbones

91. For which reason would you use a curved rectangular part with bangs on a client?
a. receding hairline
b. very strong natural part
c. prominent chin
d. round or square face

92. What type of hair can tolerate the most heat when thermal waving?
a. chemically treated hair
b. tinted hair
c. gray hair
d. fine hair

93. A strong curl with full but not maximum volume would represent which type of thermal curl?
a. volume-base curl
b. full-base curl
c. half-base curl
d. off-base curl

94. To test the temperature of curling irons, you should use
a. tissue paper.
b. a concealed lock of the client's hair.
c. your own hair.
d. your fingers.

95. Why would a cosmetologist use styling lotions or gels when blow-drying?
a. to hold the hair firmly in place
b. to make the hair dry faster
c. to avoid damage and split ends
d. to make the hair manageable

96. A thermal hair-straightening treatment lasts until the
a. client's next shampoo.
b. hair grows out.
c. hair is combed or brushed.
d. client's next haircut.

97. Before you place the pressing comb on the hair, you should test its temperature on
a. cloth or paper.
b. the client's face.
c. your hand.
d. a rubber comb.

98. The surest way to distinguish human hair from synthetic hair is to test how it
a. feels.
b. smells.
c. looks.
d. burns.

99. Because of its delicate structure and damageability, how should you clean a handmade wig?
a. on the block
b. on the client's head
c. at the dry cleaner
d. as seldom as possible

100. Which of the following is true about coloring a wig?
a. A color rinse can either lighten or darken the hair.
b. Wigs and hairpieces can be bleached just like real hair.
c. Permanent tint can be used successfully on human-hair wigs and hairpieces.
d. Semipermanent tints can be applied successfully to human-hair wigs and hairpieces.

Answers

1. a. Personal hygiene includes all the daily activities you undertake to maintain your health and cleanliness.
2. a. Although you could wear stylish shoes to work, cosmetologists, who spend most of the day on their feet, should select shoes for comfort.
3. c. Federal law requires a manufacturer to provide an MSDS (Material Safety Data Sheet) on all products used in a school or salon. It gives vital information, such as how to mix, what to do if a spill occurs, flash points, disposal, etc.
4. b. OSHA (Occupational Safety and Health Administration) was created by the U.S. Department of Labor to regulate and enforce safety and health standards in a workplace.
5. a. It is important for you to understand bacteriology so that you can help prevent the spread of diseases. (HIV is not caused by bacteria.)
6. d. Cocci, such as staphylococci and streptococci, are unable to move on their own and are usually spread through the air, through dust, or by touching infected material.
7. b. In a salon, disease can be spread by use of unsanitary tools and supplies.
8. a. In an active stage, bacteria grow and reproduce. They multiply best in places that are warm, dark, damp, and dirty.
9. d. The Material Safety Data Sheet tells you all the pertinent information including how to safely use and store the disinfectant.
10. d. Commercial cleaners may be used for ordinary cleaning, such as washing floors and countertops, but should not be used on tools.
11. d. Canities is the technical term for gray hair and is the loss of melanin pigment during the aging process.
12. b. The hair root is the part located below the skin's surface.
13. b. In cross section, wavy hair is oval.
14. c. The pH scale is the potential hydrogen in a product and measures if it is an acid or an alkaline. For example, 7+ below are acids, 7+ above are alkaline. The pH scale helps determine products used on the hair, skin, and nails.
15. b. General scalp treatments maintain healthy scalp and hair.
16. b. The client has symptoms of ringworm.
17. b. The matrix is the part of the nail structure that contains actively growing tissue.
18. d. Onychomycosis refers to a fungal infection of the nail.
19. a. Systemic illness and injury to the nail bed are the most common causes.
20. c. The skin is thinnest and most delicate over the eyelids.
21. d. A mosquito bite is a weal—an itchy, swollen lesion.
22. c. Clients with skin diseases should be referred to a doctor.
23. c. Parasites cause disease when they invade plant or animal tissue. They belong to the pathogenic category.
24. b. The muscles in the arms, legs, and face are voluntary, or striated, muscle.
25. b. This choice lists the major muscle groups of the hand.
26. a. The carotid artery and its many branches supply blood to the neck, face, and head, including the brain.
27. d. Handling electrical equipment with wet hands is an unsafe practice, because water is a conductor.
28. b. To avoid damage to the eyes, always wear safety glasses or goggles for ultraviolet therapy.
29. a. Leukonychia is a whitish discoloration of the nails caused by injury to the base of the nail.

30. b. Instant conditioners commonly contain humectants such as sorbitol and ethylene glycol.

31. d. The oxidation of melanin, caused by the action of hydrogen peroxide, causes the hair to bleach lighter.

32. a. Moisturizers create a barrier that holds the skin's natural oil and water in.

33. c. Regular hair brushing stimulates blood circulation and blood flow, and helps to loosen and remove dirt, debris, hair spray, and liquid styling tools that have built up on the scalp and shaft prior to shampooing service. It gives the hair added shine and luster.

34. b. Facial manipulators should be applied in a slow, rhythmic, even tempo. This induces relaxation.

35. b. Dry skin is due to underactive sebaceous glands because of the insufficient flow of sebum (oil).

36. a. The most successful salesperson always adapts her sales pitch to the individual client's needs and personality.

37. d. If you kept the outer towel on, it would catch the cut hair and prevent it from falling to the floor.

38. d. The purpose of applying a protective cream around the hairline is to avoid skin irritation.

39. b. Soft water is preferable for shampooing because it works up a better lather.

40. d. Brushing removes dirt and debris from the hair.

41. b. Your responsibility is to select the right shampoo for each client.

42. b. Light cured gel nails can be removed only by buffing them layer by layer and will not soak off in acetone.

43. b. Nail hardener is applied just before the base coat.

44. c. Avoid smearing polish onto the cuticles or surrounding tissues.

45. b. The hand massage will make the client's hands relaxed, flexible, and supple.

46. a. Discoloration indicates that the natural nail has developed a fungus infection.

47. d. You can only trim and file toenails. Some clients may not need a full pedicure service. If athlete's foot, corns, or infected, ingrown toenails are present, do not service them. Refer the client to a podiatrist.

48. a. Massage a muscle from the point of insertion to the point of origin.

49. d. Avoid vigorous massage of joints if your client has arthritis, because you are likely to cause the client pain.

50. a. Cosmetologists do not treat skin diseases, but they must recognize when a client should seek treatment from a doctor.

51. a. The primary purpose of facial steaming is to open the pores for deep cleansing; steaming also improves blood circulation.

52. c. Lotions containing alcohol can cause additional dryness.

53. a. Gauze is used to hold ingredients, such as crushed fruits, that would be messy if applied directly.

54. b. Use only applicators that have been sanitized or that are new and disposable.

55. b. Ask the client to smile; this will make her cheeks prominent and show where the color should be placed.

56. a. To minimize the bulging forehead, cover it with a darker shade of foundation than that used on the rest of the face.

57. b. Cutting toenails too deeply into the corners of the toes can cause ingrown nails and infection or soreness to the skin.

58. b. *Pityriasis* is the technical term for dandruff, which is an excessive production of skin cells that accumulates in clumps.

59. d. Androgenic alopecia is the term applied to male pattern baldness. It is hair loss in the fringe area usually in the shape of a horseshoe, beginning as early as teenage years and usually prominent by age 40.

60. a. Asymmetrical balance is unequal proportioning designed to balance facial features. It can be horizontal or diagonal.

61. b. Oval is considered the perfect facial shape; therefore, cosmetologists try to create that effect.

62. a. Curls that are held on base start close to the head and thus produce the greatest degree of height and fullness.

63. b. Perm the hair first, and then tint it no sooner than one week later.

64. b. Alkaline waves process at room temperature.

65. c. A patch test must be done 24–28 hours before the hair coloring is scheduled.

66. a. Cool-toned colors are those in which blue predominates.

67. c. Deposit-only hair coloring products last approximately four to six weeks.

68. b. The correct procedure is one-half inch from the scalp and work down to the ends.

69. b. A developer is an oxidizing agent that, when mixed with an oxidative haircolor, supplies the necessary oxygen gas to develop color molecules and create a change in hair color.

70. c. Because color on color makes a darker color, select a shade that is lighter than the natural hair color.

71. d. Hair lightening is a chemical process involving the diffusion of the natural color pigment or artificial color from the hair, making it appear lighter.

72. d. The Level System is a way of analyzing the darkness or lightness of a color, independent of tone.

73. d. All other colors can be achieved by mixing these three colors.

74. d. Semipermanent colors are a good choice for a client who is just beginning to go gray, because they can even out the hair tones without changing the underlying color.

75. a. A double-process application involves the use of a lightener plus a toner or a tint.

76. c. The cape must be fastened securely in the back to ensure that it doesn't slip or move during the service.

77. c. The petroleum cream base protects the client's skin and scalp and, in the case of a retouch, previously treated hair as well.

78. c. Spread the relaxer over the top and bottom of each strand with the back of a comb or with your hands.

79. a. Do not give a soft-curl perm, which uses thio, to a client whose hair has been treated with sodium hydroxide.

80. c. A good hairstyle will accentuate positive features and minimize negative ones.

81. a. Thinning hair removes excess bulk.

82. b. Straight lines are used to cut over flat surfaces on the head, and curved lines are used to cut over rounded surfaces of the head shape.

83. b. Horizontal lines are used to create one-length and low-elevation haircuts because they build weight with no graduation.

84. b. Section 2 is divided into pie-shaped wedges.

85. c. Bonding involves attaching hair wefts or single strands with an adhesive or a glue gun.

86. c. Do not comb out the waves until the hair is completely dry.

87. b. The stem of the curl gives it its mobility, action, and direction.

88. a. Stretching and applying tension results in longer-lasting curls.

89. a. The dermal papilla is cone-shaped and located at the base of the follicle, which contains the blood vessels and nerve supply responsible for the growth of the hair.

90. a. For a client with a round face, attempt to create an illusion of greater height to the face.

91. a. A curved rectangular part that sets off bangs is used for a receding hairline or very high forehead.

92. c. Hair that is gray or very coarse can tolerate the most heat.

93. b. A full-base curl is used to create a strong curl with full volume.

94. a. Use tissue paper to test the temperature of the curling irons.

95. d. Styling lotions and gels make the hair more manageable for blow-drying.

96. a. Thermal hair pressing (hair straightening) lasts only until the next shampoo.

97. a. Make sure that the pressing comb is not too hot by holding it against a piece of white cloth or paper and checking for burning.

98. d. Synthetic hair burns quickly and gives off little or no odor, in contrast to human hair, which burns slowly and gives off a very distinct odor.

99. a. Keep a handmade wig on a block at all times while you clean it.

100. d. The other statements are incorrect.

LESSON

COSMETOLOGY PRACTICE EXAM 3

LESSON SUMMARY

This is the third of four practice exams in this book that are based on the core content of your cosmetology coursework. Use this test to identify which types of questions are still giving you problems.

You are now beginning to be very familiar with the format of cosmetology exams. Your practice test-taking experience will help you most, however, if you have created a study situation as close as possible to the real testing experience.

For this third exam, simulate the official test. Find a quiet place where you will not be disturbed. Have two sharpened pencils with good erasers on hand. Complete the test in one sitting, setting a timer or a stopwatch for two hours. You should have plenty of time to answer all of the questions when you take the real exam, but you should practice working quickly, without rushing.

As before, the answer sheet is on the next page. Following the exam is the answer key, with all of the answers explained. These explanations will help you see where you need to concentrate further study. When you've finished the exam and scored it, turn back to Lesson 1 to see which questions correspond with which areas of your cosmetology coursework—then you will know which parts of your textbook to focus on before you take the fourth and final practice exam in this book.

Practice Exam 3

1.	a	b	c	d
2.	a	b	c	d
3.	a	b	c	d
4.	a	b	c	d
5.	a	b	c	d
6.	a	b	c	d
7.	a	b	c	d
8.	a	b	c	d
9.	a	b	c	d
10.	a	b	c	d
11.	a	b	c	d
12.	a	b	c	d
13.	a	b	c	d
14.	a	b	c	d
15.	a	b	c	d
16.	a	b	c	d
17.	a	b	c	d
18.	a	b	c	d
19.	a	b	c	d
20.	a	b	c	d
21.	a	b	c	d
22.	a	b	c	d
23.	a	b	c	d
24.	a	b	c	d
25.	a	b	c	d
26.	a	b	c	d
27.	a	b	c	d
28.	a	b	c	d
29.	a	b	c	d
30.	a	b	c	d
31.	a	b	c	d
32.	a	b	c	d
33.	a	b	c	d
34.	a	b	c	d
35.	a	b	c	d
36.	a	b	c	d
37.	a	b	c	d
38.	a	b	c	d
39.	a	b	c	d
40.	a	b	c	d
41.	a	b	c	d
42.	a	b	c	d
43.	a	b	c	d
44.	a	b	c	d
45.	a	b	c	d
46.	a	b	c	d
47.	a	b	c	d
48.	a	b	c	d
49.	a	b	c	d
50.	a	b	c	d
51.	a	b	c	d
52.	a	b	c	d
53.	a	b	c	d
54.	a	b	c	d
55.	a	b	c	d
56.	a	b	c	d
57.	a	b	c	d
58.	a	b	c	d
59.	a	b	c	d
60.	a	b	c	d
61.	a	b	c	d
62.	a	b	c	d
63.	a	b	c	d
64.	a	b	c	d
65.	a	b	c	d
66.	a	b	c	d
67.	a	b	c	d
68.	a	b	c	d
69.	a	b	c	d
70.	a	b	c	d
71.	a	b	c	d
72.	a	b	c	d
73.	a	b	c	d
74.	a	b	c	d
75.	a	b	c	d
76.	a	b	c	d
77.	a	b	c	d
78.	a	b	c	d
79.	a	b	c	d
80.	a	b	c	d
81.	a	b	c	d
82.	a	b	c	d
83.	a	b	c	d
84.	a	b	c	d
85.	a	b	c	d
86.	a	b	c	d
87.	a	b	c	d
88.	a	b	c	d
89.	a	b	c	d
90.	a	b	c	d
91.	a	b	c	d
92.	a	b	c	d
93.	a	b	c	d
94.	a	b	c	d
95.	a	b	c	d
96.	a	b	c	d
97.	a	b	c	d
98.	a	b	c	d
99.	a	b	c	d
100.	a	b	c	d

Practice Exam 3

1. Each year, many workers, including cosmetologists, report problems with carpal tunnel, tendonitis, and back injuries. These disorders are known as
  a. health issues.
  b. musculoskeletal disorders.
  c. cosmetological disorders.
  d. posture disorders.

2. The study of human characteristics related to a specific work environment is called
  a. stress.
  b. physical presentation.
  c. ergonomics.
  d. personal hygiene.

3. Part of effective communication skills for a cosmetologist includes
  a. telling the client what's best for him or her.
  b. avoiding needless talking while at work.
  c. understanding what the client wants.
  d. ignoring the client's wishes while seeming to listen politely.

4. ________________________ is referred as a professional image made up of posture, walk, and movements.
  a. Physical presentation
  b. Ergonomics
  c. Posture control
  d. Professional attitude

5. Which of the following bacteria cause abscesses, boils, and pustules?
  a. streptococci
  b. diplococci
  c. treponema
  d. staphylococci

6. Which disease is caused by a virus?
  a. tuberculosis
  b. the common cold
  c. strep throat
  d. pediculosis

7. How can you prevent the spread of infection in the salon?
  a. Sterilize all equipment and furniture between clients.
  b. Practice good personal hygiene and sanitation.
  c. Drink large amounts of water and eat a healthy diet.
  d. Take a multivitamin.

8. Which of the following lives only by penetrating cells and becoming part of them?
  a. virus
  b. bacteria
  c. organisms
  d. amoebas

9. Which disinfectant is nontoxic, odorless, fast acting, and used to disinfect implements?
  a. 70% alcohol
  b. phenal
  c. quat
  d. 5% bleach

10. What is the average growth of hair per month?
  a. $\frac{1}{8}$ inch
  b. $\frac{1}{4}$ inch
  c. $\frac{1}{2}$ inch
  d. $\frac{3}{4}$ inch

11. What part of the hair is located below the scalp?
a. hair root
b. hair shaft
c. trichology
d. arrector pili muscle

12. The tubelike opening in the skin or scalp that surrounds the hair root is referred to as the
a. epidermis.
b. dermis.
c. papilla.
d. follicle.

13. The direction of hair growth is referred to as a
a. cowlick.
b. natural part.
c. whorl.
d. hair stream.

14. Which of the following refers to the hair shaft's ability to absorb moisture?
a. porosity
b. elasticity
c. viscosity
d. pigmentation

15. Hair growth slows rapidly at what age?
a. 30
b. 40
c. 50
d. 60

16. The part of the hair that extends above the skin surface is called the
a. hair shaft.
b. hair root.
c. follicle.
d. sebaceous gland.

17. The extension of the cuticle over the half moon at the base of the nail is referred to as the
a. lunula.
b. mantle.
c. eponychium.
d. perionychium.

18. __________ causes white spots in the nail.
a. Poor nutrition
b. Poor circulation
c. Minor injury
d. Fungus infection

19. When you are doing a manicure on a client, your orangewood stick and emery board cannot be sanitized. What do you do with them?
a. Put them in your manicure drawer.
b. Put them in your pocket.
c. Place them in disinfectant.
d. Give them to the client.

20. The point where the natural nail plate meets the artificial nail tip before it is glued to the natural nail is called the
a. position stop.
b. lunula.
c. position go.
d. matrix.

21. The cracks in a client's skin caused by dry and chapped hands are called
a. excoriations.
b. fissures.
c. scars.
d. ulcers.

22. How often should nail-enhancement services be balanced or filled in?
a. every one to two weeks
b. every two to three weeks
c. every five days
d. every six weeks

23. The skin and scalp are both examples of
a. muscular tissue.
b. connective tissue.
c. nerve tissue.
d. epithelial tissue.

24. Which of the following does NOT stimulate muscle tissue?
a. application of heat
b. application of cold
c. massage
d. electric current

25. The chief sensory nerve of the face is the
a. fourth cranial nerve.
b. fifth cranial nerve.
c. sixth cranial nerve.
d. seventh cranial nerve.

26. The main blood supply to the arm and hand flows through the
a. infraorbital and frontal arteries.
b. radial and ulnar arteries.
c. vena cava and aorta.
d. carotid artery.

27. Your hair dryer has tripped a circuit breaker. You reset the circuit breaker, but the dryer immediately breaks the circuit once again. The safest thing to do is to
a. call an electrician to locate the problem.
b. connect the appliance to another circuit.
c. use a coin to complete the circuit.
d. attempt to rewire the appliance.

28. In electrolysis the electric current is applied with a very fine, needle-shaped electrode that is inserted into each
a. cell.
b. hair follicle.
c. hair strand.
d. capillary.

29. The pH of normal hair is approximately
a. 3.5
b. 5.0
c. 6.5
d. 8.0

30. Which type of conditioner enters the cortex of the hair and replaces the keratin lost during chemical services?
a. instant conditioner
b. moisturizing conditioner
c. protein conditioner
d. hot oil conditioner

31. Which statement about color fillers is correct?
a. Fillers are used before chemical services to increase the hair's porosity.
b. Fillers attach to the carbohydrate component of the hair.
c. Fillers occupy the spaces left in the hair shaft after the diffusion of melanin.
d. Fillers are made exclusively of human-hair derivatives.

32. The two categories of facial treatments are
a. melodic and corrective.
b. preservative and harmonious.
c. corrective and preservative.
d. melodic and preservative.

33. How many bones are located in the cranium?
a. 6
b. 8
c. 10
d. 15

34. The four basic haircuts in hairstyling are blunt, layers, long layers, and
a. short layers.
b. 90° layers.
c. graduated.
d. weight line.

35. A client should be greeted by the ____________. This affects the client's impression of your salon.
a. owner
b. cosmetologist
c. manicurist
d. receptionist

36. When you use the scissors-over-comb technique to cut hair, what is your guide?
a. your fingers
b. the back of your head
c. the scissors
d. the barber comb

37. Why is it necessary to place a towel over the client's gown when draping for chemical services?
a. to protect the client's skin and clothing
b. to prevent the client from becoming chilly
c. to allow the client's clipped hair to fall to the floor
d. to make the client look more attractive

38. What is needed when draping a client for a dry-hair service?
a. neck strip only
b. neck strip and cape
c. towel only
d. two towels, neck strip, and cape

39. When selecting a shampoo for a client, you should choose one that
a. suits the client's hair type.
b. uses only natural ingredients.
c. will eliminate dandruff.
d. smells great.

40. The correct procedure for adjusting water temperature before shampooing is to
a. turn on the hot water first and gradually add cold water.
b. turn on both hot and cold water simultaneously.
c. turn on the cold water first and then adjust the hot water.
d. use a thermometer to obtain the client's preferred temperature.

41. The visible line that separates colored hair from newly grown hair is called
a. hyperpigmentation.
b. hypopigmentation.
c. line of demarcation.
d. line of decolorization.

42. Habitual use of cream rinses can
a. make the hair healthy and lustrous.
b. serve in place of chemical treatments.
c. correct the pH of the scalp.
d. make hair heavy and oily.

43. When should you clean your manicuring table?
a. when a new client arrives and sits down
b. after every three clients
c. right after each manicure
d. at the end of your shift

44. Before shaping a client's nails, you should
a. discuss what shape the client desires.
b. tell the client the shape and colors you prefer.
c. soften the client's cuticles.
d. clean and bleach the free edges of the nails.

45. An oil manicure is beneficial for clients with brittle nails and
a. dry cuticles.
b. vitamin deficiencies.
c. nail diseases.
d. dry, patchy skin on the hands.

46. How can you prevent a fungal infection from growing underneath a sculptured nail?
a. Wear rubber gloves while giving all manicures.
b. Avoid touching the nail after the acrylic primer is applied.
c. Sterilize the nail bed with alcohol or peroxide.
d. Tell the client to avoid hand washing for 48 hours after nail sculpturing.

47. Which of the following is a result of filing into the corners of your client's toenails?
a. faster nail growth
b. ingrown toenails
c. corns
d. bunions

48. The massage movement described as a light, continuous stroking movement is
a. petrissage.
b. friction.
c. effleurage.
d. percussion.

49. Massage benefits the skin and the underlying structures because its general effect is to
a. speed up the digestive process.
b. make the client feel sleepy.
c. stimulate bodily activity in the region.
d. increase sensitivity to pain and fatigue.

50. The process of removing bulk from hair without removing length is called
a. texturing.
b. spinning.
c. thinning.
d. sliding.

51. Which part of a curl gives direction and movement?
a. base
b. stem
c. circle
d. ends

52. You have used only half of a mask product that comes packaged for one-time use. You should
a. use the other half for the next client.
b. discard the remaining product.
c. sell the remaining product.
d. take the remainder home for your own use.

53. Which one of the following types of pin curls gives the most mobility?
a. no-stem curl
b. half-stem curl
c. on-base curl
d. full-stem curl

54. In roller placement, which base gives the least amount of volume?
a. on-base
b. half off
c. three-quarters off
d. off-base

55. Extensions should be attached at what distance from the front hairline, sides, and nape?
a. 4 inches
b. 3 inches
c. 2 inches
d. 1 inch

56. In which method are hair extensions secured at the base of the client's own hair by sewing?
a. sew-and-cut method
b. track-and-knot method
c. track-and-sew method
d. cut-and-track method

57. Semipermanent individual eyelashes (also called eye tabbing) last approximately
a. one week.
b. two to four weeks.
c. four to six weeks.
d. six to eight weeks.

58. Teasing, ratting, matting, and French lacing refer to
a. slicing.
b. wrapping.
c. back combing.
d. front combing.

59. A method of waving and curling straight hair with a special iron is called
a. thermal waving.
b. conventional waving.
c. permanent waving.
d. ridge waving.

60. The purpose of the neutralizers used in permanent waving is to
a. break down the hair's structure.
b. reduce the amount of heat needed.
c. create a very tight curl.
d. reharden the hair and fix it into a curl.

61. The purpose of preperm shampooing is to
a. thoroughly wet the hair.
b. remove residues that might prevent the waving lotion from penetrating.
c. remove all chemicals that might neutralize the waving lotion.
d. soften the outer keratin coating.

62. Which hair-texture type is fragile, easy to process, and easier to damage?
a. resistant
b. normal
c. limp
d. coarse

63. When would you not perform thermal ironing?
a. on virgin hair
b. on blown-dry hair
c. on permanent-waved hair
d. on relaxed hair

64. How would you give a client a partial perm?
   a. Leave the lotion on for half the normal time.
   b. Do only the section of the head desired by the client.
   c. Wind the rods up only partway.
   d. Use very large rods.

65. The purpose of a strand test is to determine
   a. whether any pretreatment is needed.
   b. whether the client is allergic to the tint.
   c. how the final result will look.
   d. how the chosen tint looks in artificial light.

66. Your client complains about her brassy hair color. To neutralize her unwanted highlights, you should use a product that contains
   a. orange.
   b. red.
   c. black.
   d. blue.

67. Which of the following is an example of a natural coloring agent?
   a. metallic hair dye
   b. compound dye
   c. henna
   d. peroxide

68. The purpose of a finishing rinse after coloring hair with a lightener and toner is to close the cuticle and to
   a. stop the lightening process.
   b. achieve the desired color.
   c. adjust the hair's pH.
   d. add blonde highlights.

69. When applying a presoftener, the correct procedure is to process for
   a. 2–5 minutes at room temperature.
   b. 5–20 minutes at room temperature.
   c. 2–5 minutes with heat.
   d. 5–20 minutes with heat.

70. When a colorist refers to a contributing pigment, he or she means the
   a. client's natural hair color and tone.
   b. client's desired hair color and tone.
   c. combination of tints that make up the color product.
   d. semipermanent hair color that is added last.

71. When working with aniline-derived products, you should protect yourself from allergic reactions by wearing
   a. goggles.
   b. a face mask.
   c. gloves.
   d. a disposable gown.

72. The relative strength of warm or cool tones in the hair is referred to as
   a. tone.
   b. intensity.
   c. depth.
   d. highlighting.

73. Secondary colors are created by mixing
   a. a primary and a secondary color.
   b. two primary colors in equal proportion.
   c. all three primary colors in equal proportion.
   d. a primary and a tertiary color in equal proportion.

74. Which statement about the effect of henna on the hair is correct?
a. Henna can be used to obtain bright red shades only.
b. Henna makes conditioners penetrate the hair more easily.
c. Henna can make fine hair appear thicker and more lustrous.
d. Henna does not penetrate the hair's cortex layer.

75. A pastel color that is applied only after prelightening is a
a. tint.
b. toner.
c. solvent.
d. stabilizer.

76. Temporarily straightening extremely curly and unruly hair refers to
a. thermal hair straightening.
b. thermal hair curling.
c. chemically relaxing.
d. chemically permanent waving.

77. The three steps in chemical hair relaxing are
a. lather, rinse, repeat.
b. apply, wait, remove.
c. presoften, condition, neutralize.
d. process, neutralize, condition.

78. What water temperature should be used when rinsing the relaxer out of a client's hair?
a. cold
b. between cool and tepid
c. warm
d. very hot

79. When you are performing a blunt cut, you are
a. cutting all hair on the head to the same length.
b. cutting a strand of hair straight across.
c. slithering.
d. layering.

80. When you cut the hair at an elevation of below 90°, you are
a. removing weight.
b. building weight.
c. removing bulk.
d. thinning hair.

81. What are two types of guidelines used in cutting?
a. stationary and traveling
b. traveling and returning
c. stationary and returning
d. traveling and inactive

82. A point on the head that marks where the surface of the head changes or the behavior of the hair changes is called
a. a reference point.
b. a cutting point.
c. a guiding point.
d. a scissor point.

83. Combing the hair away from its natural falling position, rather than straight out from the head, and cutting it toward a guideline to create a length increase in the design is called
a. under cutting.
b. over cutting.
c. under direction.
d. over direction.

84. Determining the number of individual hair strands on one square inch of scalp and describing it as thin, medium, or thick is identifying the hair's
a. perimeter.
b. volume.
c. elasticity.
d. density.

85. What is hair texture?
a. the amount of movement in the hair
b. the general quality and feel of the hair
c. the amount of water the hair can absorb
d. the length that the hair can stretch

86. What is wave pattern?
a. the amount of movement in the hair
b. the general quality and feel of the hair
c. the amount of water the hair can absorb
d. the length that the hair can stretch

87. To create short tapers, short haircuts, fades, and flat-top styles, which of the following tools is best used?
a. thinning shears
b. edgers
c. straight razor
d. clippers

88. The pigment that is contained in the hair's cortex and determines natural hair color is
a. melatonin.
b. keratin.
c. melanin.
d. keratonin.

89. The purpose of all-over layering of long hair is to
a. thin the hair and make it look neater.
b. add volume and bounce.
c. eliminate split ends.
d. make the hair less curly.

90. A hairstyle for a client with a pear-shaped face should be
a. long and narrow.
b. wide on top.
c. full and high.
d. asymmetrical.

91. An artificial covering made up of a network of interwoven hair that completely covers a client's natural hair is a
a. braid.
b. wig.
c. fall.
d. weave.

92. The comb used with a thermal iron should be made of
a. hard rubber and have fine teeth.
b. plastic and have fine teeth.
c. bone and have fine teeth.
d. plastic and have coarse teeth.

93. Which type of curl has only slight lift or volume?
a. volume-base curl
b. full-base curl
c. half-base curl
d. off-base curl

94. What should a cosmetologist do after completing each curl during a thermal setting?
  a. Comb it out loosely.
  b. Apply clear lacquer.
  c. Apply setting gel or lotion.
  d. Clip it to its base.

95. During blow-drying, hot air is directed
  a. from the scalp toward the hair ends.
  b. straight toward the scalp.
  c. upward from the back of the neck.
  d. downward at all times.

96. Which type of hair requires the least heat and pressure for thermal straightening?
  a. wiry hair
  b. fine hair
  c. medium hair
  d. coarse hair

97. __________________ is the technique of taking natural textured hair that is intertwined and mashed together to form a single network of hair without the use of chemicals.
  a. Braiding
  b. Locking
  c. Rope braiding
  d. Inverted braiding

98. When a folded piece of paper is placed on the ends of the hair during permanent waving, this is called a(n)
  a. end paper.
  b. bookend paper wrap.
  c. single flat paper wrap.
  d. double flat paper wrap.

99. Another name for a straight set wrap in permanent waving is a
  a. basic perm wrap.
  b. bricklay perm wrap.
  c. spiral perm wrap.
  d. curvature perm wrap.

100. In hair color, a developer is mixed with the color to begin oxidizing or processing. What is the most common developer used?
  a. ammonia
  b. hydrogen peroxide
  c. analine
  d. water

Answers

1. b. Workplace disorders such as carpal tunnel, tendonitis, and back injuries are also called musculoskeletal disorders, or MSDs. They are caused by the way you stand and improper movements and body posture.
2. c. Ergonomics is the study of human characteristics related to specific work environments.
3. c. An important part of effective communication skills for a cosmetologist is understanding the client's wishes.
4. a. Physical presentation consists of posture and walk. Do you hold up your shoulders and back and convey confidence, or do you slouch? Good physical presentation enhances your professional image.
5. d. Staphylococci cause skin infections such as abscesses and boils.
6. b. Colds are caused by extremely tiny viruses.
7. b. Personal hygiene and basic sanitation techniques can prevent the spread of infection in the salon.
8. a. A virus lives only by penetrating cells and becoming part of them, while bacteria are organisms that can live on their own.
9. c. Quat, or quaternary ammonium compounds, is a nontoxic, odorless, fast-acting disinfectant.
10. c. On average, hair grows $\frac{1}{2}$ inch per month. Growth varies depending on gender, age, and location on the body.
11. a. The hair root is located below the scalp. Its structures are the follicle bulb, papula, arrector pili muscle, and sebaceous glands.
12. d. The follicle is the depression in the skin or scalp out of which the hair shaft grows.
13. d. The natural direction of hair growth is referred to as the hair stream.
14. a. Porosity refers to the ability of the hair to absorb moisture.
15. c. At age 50, hair growth slows down rapidly. Also, women's hair grows faster than men's.
16. a. The hair shaft extends above the skin surface.
17. c. The eponychium is the part of the cuticle that extends over the base of the nail.
18. c. White spots are usually caused by previous minor injury to the nail bed.
19. d. You should give the implements to the client to take home and use, or break them in half and throw them away.
20. a. The position stop is the point where the natural nail tip meets the artificial tip before it is glued on.
21. b. A fissure is a crack that penetrates into the dermis.
22. b. Every two to three weeks nail enhancement services should be balanced or filled in for new growth at the base of the natural nail. If they are not refilled or rebalanced, the client can get lifting of the acrylic product, which will cause moisture, dirt, debris, and food to become trapped and bacteria to possibly set in. Change in color could indicate bacterial growth.
23. d. Epithelial tissue, which includes the skin, scalp, and mucous membranes, is the body's protective covering.
24. b. Muscles are stimulated by heat, electric current, light, and massage, but not by cold.
25. b. The fifth cranial nerve is the major sensory nerve of the face.
26. b. The radial and ulnar arteries supply blood to the arm and hand.
27. a. If a circuit breaker trips the circuit again, immediately call an electrician to locate the problem.
28. b. In electrolysis, the current is applied with a very fine, needle-shaped electrode that is inserted into each hair follicle.

29. b. The pH of normal hair is approximately 4.5 to 5.5; in other words, normal human hair is slightly acidic.

30. c. Protein conditioners are designed to enter the hair shaft and repair damage.

31. c. Fillers, which are made of inexpensive protein products, take up the spaces left in the hair after the diffusion of melanin and, thus, correct its porosity.

32. c. Facial treatments fall under two categories: preservative and corrective. A preservative treatment is meant to maintain the health of the facial skin, and a corrective treatment is meant to correct facial skin conditions.

33. b. Eight bones are located in the cranium. They are an occipital bone, two pariental bones, a frontal bone, two temporal bones, an ethnoid bone, and a sphenoid bone.

34. c. In haircutting, there are variations on the four basic types of haircuts, which are beneficial for experimenting with designing in haircutting. A *graduated* cut, also called a *wedge* or *stacked* cut, is done at a 45° angle. The *blunt* cut is a one-length cut done at a 0° angle. In a *layered* cut, the lengths are achieved with elevation or over direction of the hair, usually at a 90° angle. In a *long layer* cut, done at a 180° angle, shorter layers at the top of the head and longer layers toward the nape give more volume to the hair.

35. d. The receptionist should be courteous and friendly and should call clients by name.

36. d. The barber comb is the guide used to cut. Hold the barber comb by the large end and keep scissors and comb together as you cut and move up the head. This is also called shingling.

37. a. You fold and secure a towel over the gown to protect the client's skin and clothing.

38. b. For dry hair services, such as a comb-out, use a neck strip and cape only.

39. a. Select the shampoo based on your client's hair type.

40. c. The safest procedure is to turn on the cold water first and then adjust the hot water.

41. c. The line of demarcation is the visible line that separates colored hair from newly grown hair.

42. d. Habitual use of cream rinses can make the hair heavy and oily, leading to increased shampooing and further hair damage.

43. c. So that the manicure table is always ready for a new client, clean it immediately after you complete a manicure.

44. a. Always discuss with the client what nail shape he or she wants.

45. a. An oil manicure is beneficial for clients who have brittle or ridged nails or dry cuticles.

46. b. Because the primer contains antiseptics to prevent the growth of fungus, avoid touching the nail after you apply the primer.

47. b. File the toenails straight across to avoid ingrown nails.

48. c. Effleurage is a light, continuous stroking movement.

49. c. Massage stimulates all local activity, including circulation, muscle tone, and secretions from skin glands.

50. a. Texturing is the technique of removing bulk without removing length. It produces wispy and/or spiky effects, adds volume, and makes hair move. Notching, point cutting, slicing, and carving are examples of texturizing with shears.

51. b. The stem is the section of a curl that gives it direction and movement. It is located between the base and the circle of a curl.

52. b. To avoid the risk of contamination, you should always discard disposable supplies after each facial.

53. d. Full-stem curl is placed completely off base and has the greatest mobility.

54. d. Off-base roller placement gives the least volume. Hold the hair at 45° to roll down and place the roller completely off base.

55. d. No hair extensions should ever be any closer than one inch from the front hairline, sides, and nape area.

56. c. In the track-and-sew method, hair extensions are secured at the base of the client's own hair by sewing and the hair is attached to an on-the-scalp braid, which serves as the track.

57. d. These lashes, which are attached to individual natural lashes, fall out along with the natural lashes and last approximately six to eight weeks.

58. c. Teasing, ratting, matting, and French lacing refer to back combing. These are ways to increase volume and height in hair designing.

59. a. Thermal waving, also called marcel waving or thermal curling, is a method of curling hair.

60. d. Without a neutralizer, the hair shape would revert after one or two shampoos.

61. b. Pre-perm shampooing must remove all residues and coatings that might prevent the waving lotion from penetrating the hair strands.

62. c. Fragile, easy-to-process, easier-to-damage hair indicates the client has fine, limp hair texture.

63. d. You would not perform thermal ironing on chemically relaxed hair because it causes breakage.

64. b. A partial perm perms only the section of the head desired by the client.

65. c. The purpose of a strand test is to determine how the final result will look.

66. d. Blue, the complementary color to orange, will neutralize unwanted orange tones.

67. c. Henna is a natural, plant-based product.

68. c. The finishing rinse is needed to adjust the hair's acidity because toners are highly alkaline.

69. b. The correct procedure is 5–20 minutes at room temperature.

70. a. The contributing pigment is the client's underlying hair color.

71. c. Wear gloves at all times when working with aniline-derived products.

72. b. The relative strength of the warm or cool tones is intensity.

73. b. Secondary colors are created by mixing two primary colors in equal proportion.

74. c. Because henna coats the surface of the hair, it can make fine hair appear thicker and more lustrous.

75. b. A toner is a pastel hair color that is applied after prelightening.

76. a. Thermal hair straightening or hair pressing temporarily straightens extremely curly or unruly hair with the aid of a heated iron or comb. The three types are soft press, medium press, and hard press.

77. d. The three basic steps are process, neutralize, and condition.

78. c. Cold or cool water will not stop the relaxing process, and very hot water will irritate the client's scalp.

79. b. Blunt cutting means cutting each strand of hair straight across, without slithering.

80. b. You will build weight when you elevate the hair below 90° in a haircut.

81. a. The two types of guidelines are stationary, which do not move about the head, and traveling, which are used to ensure that each section in a particular part of the head is cut evenly.

82. a. The reference point marks a surface on the head where the behavior of the hair changes, which indicates to the cutter a place where his technique may need to be altered.

83. d. Over direction occurs when you comb the hair away from its natural falling position, rather than straight out from the head, toward a guideline; it is used in graduated and layered haircuts to create a length increase in the design.

84. d. Hair density is the number of individual hair strands on one square inch of scalp and is usually described as thin, medium, or thick.

85. a. Hair texture is the general quality and feel of the hair and is usually classified as coarse, medium, and fine.

86. b. The wave pattern is the amount of movement in the hair strand and is usually classified as stick-straight hair, wavy hair, curly hair, extremely curly hair, or anything in between.

87. d. Electric clippers make creating short tapers, short haircuts, fades, and flat-tops easy and efficient.

88. c. The cortex contains the natural pigment called melanin, which determines natural hair color. There are two types of melanin in the cortex: Eumelanin is the melanin that gives black and brown color to hair, and pheomelanin is the melanin found in red hair.

89. b. All-over layering adds volume and swing to long hair.

90. c. A high, full style will camouflage the facial shape.

91. b. A wig can be defined as an artificial covering for the head consisting of a network of interwoven hair that completely covers the client's natural hair and is mainly used for covering up hair loss from aging or disease or to temporarily change the client's look.

92. a. The comb should be made of a nonflammable material, such as hard rubber; fine teeth hold the hair more firmly.

93. d. An off-base curl provides only slight lift or volume.

94. d. Clip each curl to its base until the whole head is completed.

95. a. During blow-drying, the hot air is directed from the scalp toward the hair ends, not directly toward the scalp.

96. b. Fine hair requires the least heat and pressure to be thermally straightened.

97. b. Locks or dreadlocks is the technique of intertwined hair to form a single or separate network of hair. These grow in several slow stages, which can take six months to a year depending on length, density, and coil patterns of the hair.

98. b. When you are rolling hair for a permanent wave, bookend paper wrap is used on short hair and placed with the hair sandwiched between. Avoid bunching the hair or getting hair into the fold.

99. a. In a basic perm wrap, you have nine sections and each section is rolled down. All bases for rods are horizontal and are half off base.

100. b. Hydrogen peroxide (H_2O_2) is used as an oxidizing agent or developer.

LESSON

COSMETOLOGY PRACTICE EXAM 4

LESSON SUMMARY

This is the last of four practice exams in this book that are based on the core content of your cosmetology coursework. Using all of the experience and strategy that you gained from the other three exams and from the Refresher Course, take this test to gauge how much you have learned and retained using this book.

Although this is the last practice exam, it is not designed to be any harder or trickier than the other three. It is simply another representation of what you can expect to find on the official Cosmetology Exam. There shouldn't be anything here to surprise you. In fact, you probably will feel very comfortable with the exam. That's the idea for the real test, too—you won't be surprised, so you won't be unprepared.

For this last test, pull together all the tips you've been practicing since the first test. Give yourself the time and the space to work—perhaps in an unfamiliar location such as a library, since you won't be taking the official exam in your living room. In addition, draw on what you've learned from reading the answer explanations. Remember the types of questions that tripped you up in the past, and when you are unsure, try to consider how these answers were explained.

Most of all, relax. You have worked hard and have every right to be confident!

The answer sheet is on the following page, followed by the exam. The correct answers, each fully explained, follow the exam. When you have read and understood all the answers, turn back to Lesson 1 for an explanation of how to score and analyze your exam. You will then determine possible weak areas to study further in Lesson 4, the Cosmetology Refresher Course.

Practice Exam 4

1.	ⓐ	ⓑ	ⓒ	ⓓ	36.	ⓐ	ⓑ	ⓒ	ⓓ	71.	ⓐ	ⓑ	ⓒ	ⓓ
2.	ⓐ	ⓑ	ⓒ	ⓓ	37.	ⓐ	ⓑ	ⓒ	ⓓ	72.	ⓐ	ⓑ	ⓒ	ⓓ
3.	ⓐ	ⓑ	ⓒ	ⓓ	38.	ⓐ	ⓑ	ⓒ	ⓓ	73.	ⓐ	ⓑ	ⓒ	ⓓ
4.	ⓐ	ⓑ	ⓒ	ⓓ	39.	ⓐ	ⓑ	ⓒ	ⓓ	74.	ⓐ	ⓑ	ⓒ	ⓓ
5.	ⓐ	ⓑ	ⓒ	ⓓ	40.	ⓐ	ⓑ	ⓒ	ⓓ	75.	ⓐ	ⓑ	ⓒ	ⓓ
6.	ⓐ	ⓑ	ⓒ	ⓓ	41.	ⓐ	ⓑ	ⓒ	ⓓ	76.	ⓐ	ⓑ	ⓒ	ⓓ
7.	ⓐ	ⓑ	ⓒ	ⓓ	42.	ⓐ	ⓑ	ⓒ	ⓓ	77.	ⓐ	ⓑ	ⓒ	ⓓ
8.	ⓐ	ⓑ	ⓒ	ⓓ	43.	ⓐ	ⓑ	ⓒ	ⓓ	78.	ⓐ	ⓑ	ⓒ	ⓓ
9.	ⓐ	ⓑ	ⓒ	ⓓ	44.	ⓐ	ⓑ	ⓒ	ⓓ	79.	ⓐ	ⓑ	ⓒ	ⓓ
10.	ⓐ	ⓑ	ⓒ	ⓓ	45.	ⓐ	ⓑ	ⓒ	ⓓ	80.	ⓐ	ⓑ	ⓒ	ⓓ
11.	ⓐ	ⓑ	ⓒ	ⓓ	46.	ⓐ	ⓑ	ⓒ	ⓓ	81.	ⓐ	ⓑ	ⓒ	ⓓ
12.	ⓐ	ⓑ	ⓒ	ⓓ	47.	ⓐ	ⓑ	ⓒ	ⓓ	82.	ⓐ	ⓑ	ⓒ	ⓓ
13.	ⓐ	ⓑ	ⓒ	ⓓ	48.	ⓐ	ⓑ	ⓒ	ⓓ	83.	ⓐ	ⓑ	ⓒ	ⓓ
14.	ⓐ	ⓑ	ⓒ	ⓓ	49.	ⓐ	ⓑ	ⓒ	ⓓ	84.	ⓐ	ⓑ	ⓒ	ⓓ
15.	ⓐ	ⓑ	ⓒ	ⓓ	50.	ⓐ	ⓑ	ⓒ	ⓓ	85.	ⓐ	ⓑ	ⓒ	ⓓ
16.	ⓐ	ⓑ	ⓒ	ⓓ	51.	ⓐ	ⓑ	ⓒ	ⓓ	86.	ⓐ	ⓑ	ⓒ	ⓓ
17.	ⓐ	ⓑ	ⓒ	ⓓ	52.	ⓐ	ⓑ	ⓒ	ⓓ	87.	ⓐ	ⓑ	ⓒ	ⓓ
18.	ⓐ	ⓑ	ⓒ	ⓓ	53.	ⓐ	ⓑ	ⓒ	ⓓ	88.	ⓐ	ⓑ	ⓒ	ⓓ
19.	ⓐ	ⓑ	ⓒ	ⓓ	54.	ⓐ	ⓑ	ⓒ	ⓓ	89.	ⓐ	ⓑ	ⓒ	ⓓ
20.	ⓐ	ⓑ	ⓒ	ⓓ	55.	ⓐ	ⓑ	ⓒ	ⓓ	90.	ⓐ	ⓑ	ⓒ	ⓓ
21.	ⓐ	ⓑ	ⓒ	ⓓ	56.	ⓐ	ⓑ	ⓒ	ⓓ	91.	ⓐ	ⓑ	ⓒ	ⓓ
22.	ⓐ	ⓑ	ⓒ	ⓓ	57.	ⓐ	ⓑ	ⓒ	ⓓ	92.	ⓐ	ⓑ	ⓒ	ⓓ
23.	ⓐ	ⓑ	ⓒ	ⓓ	58.	ⓐ	ⓑ	ⓒ	ⓓ	93.	ⓐ	ⓑ	ⓒ	ⓓ
24.	ⓐ	ⓑ	ⓒ	ⓓ	59.	ⓐ	ⓑ	ⓒ	ⓓ	94.	ⓐ	ⓑ	ⓒ	ⓓ
25.	ⓐ	ⓑ	ⓒ	ⓓ	60.	ⓐ	ⓑ	ⓒ	ⓓ	95.	ⓐ	ⓑ	ⓒ	ⓓ
26.	ⓐ	ⓑ	ⓒ	ⓓ	61.	ⓐ	ⓑ	ⓒ	ⓓ	96.	ⓐ	ⓑ	ⓒ	ⓓ
27.	ⓐ	ⓑ	ⓒ	ⓓ	62.	ⓐ	ⓑ	ⓒ	ⓓ	97.	ⓐ	ⓑ	ⓒ	ⓓ
28.	ⓐ	ⓑ	ⓒ	ⓓ	63.	ⓐ	ⓑ	ⓒ	ⓓ	98.	ⓐ	ⓑ	ⓒ	ⓓ
29.	ⓐ	ⓑ	ⓒ	ⓓ	64.	ⓐ	ⓑ	ⓒ	ⓓ	99.	ⓐ	ⓑ	ⓒ	ⓓ
30.	ⓐ	ⓑ	ⓒ	ⓓ	65.	ⓐ	ⓑ	ⓒ	ⓓ	100.	ⓐ	ⓑ	ⓒ	ⓓ
31.	ⓐ	ⓑ	ⓒ	ⓓ	66.	ⓐ	ⓑ	ⓒ	ⓓ					
32.	ⓐ	ⓑ	ⓒ	ⓓ	67.	ⓐ	ⓑ	ⓒ	ⓓ					
33.	ⓐ	ⓑ	ⓒ	ⓓ	68.	ⓐ	ⓑ	ⓒ	ⓓ					
34.	ⓐ	ⓑ	ⓒ	ⓓ	69.	ⓐ	ⓑ	ⓒ	ⓓ					
35.	ⓐ	ⓑ	ⓒ	ⓓ	70.	ⓐ	ⓑ	ⓒ	ⓓ					

Practice Exam 4

1. To work in a salon, the cosmetologist must be free from
a. arthritis.
b. canitus.
c. nonpathogenic bacteria.
d. contagious disease.

2. Good posture is important to cosmetologists both to improve personal appearance as well as to
a. command a higher salary.
b. prevent fatigue and physical problems.
c. increase self-confidence.
d. promote and strengthen self-discipline.

3. Sanitized implements are best stored
a. in an open box.
b. in a closed, clean, dry container.
c. in an open, clean, dry container.
d. on a shelf.

4. Microbacterium, or fortuitum furunculosis, is a rod-shaped bacterium that is normally harmless but can cause serious infections if the manufacturer's sanitation procedures are not followed after what service?
a. pedicure done with a tub
b. pedicure done with a foot bath
c. pedicure done with a whirlpool foot spa
d. pedicure done with a dishpan

5. Short, rod-shaped bacteria are referred to as
a. bacilli.
b. cocci.
c. spirilla.
d. streptococci.

6. Scabies is caused by a
a. virus.
b. bacterium.
c. louse.
d. mite.

7. HIV can be spread in all of the following ways EXCEPT
a. sexual intercourse.
b. sharing needles.
c. blood transfusions.
d. shaking hands.

8. An important rule of sanitation is to
a. reuse client gowns or headbands only three times before washing.
b. wash your hands after using the restroom and between clients.
c. store pins, rollers, and other tools in your pockets.
d. make sure clients' pets are kept near them and not allowed to roam freely.

9. A client has an open sore on her scalp. You should work on her hair only if
a. her doctor certifies that it is not infectious.
b. she assures you that it is safe.
c. you cover the sore with a bandage.
d. she insists that she cannot come back another day.

10. For hand washing, salons should provide
a. disinfectants.
b. liquid antiseptic soaps.
c. antibacterial bar soaps.
d. formalin.

11. Hepatitis is a virus transmitted through body fluids and the blood or by a cut or sore on the skin. What other virus is this similar to?
a. HIV
b. venereal disease
c. systemic disease
d. occupational disease

12. Sebaceous glands in the scalp and skin produce
a. sweat.
b. dandruff.
c. oil.
d. keratin.

13. What should the label of a disinfectant say to ensure that it will be effective against virus-causing organisms in your salon?
a. 70% alcohol, not EPA registered
b. quat EPA registered
c. contains phenols
d. hospital-grade disinfectant with virucide and tuberculocide, EPA registered

14. The hair's pigment, or color, is found in its
a. epidermis.
b. cortex.
c. medulla.
d. cuticle.

15. The art of shaping and molding the hair into an S pattern using fingers, comb, and waving lotion is
a. skip wave.
b. pin curls.
c. finger wave.
d. bouffant.

16. Hair is made of the same protein as the
a. teeth.
b. bones.
c. nails.
d. muscles.

17. The average nail grows approximately how fast?
a. $\frac{1}{8}$ inch per week
b. $\frac{1}{4}$ inch per week
c. $\frac{1}{8}$ inch per month
d. $\frac{1}{4}$ inch per month

18. A patch test is NOT necessary for a
a. semipermanent color.
b. permanent color.
c. tint retouch.
d. temporary color.

19. What advice would you give to a client with badly bitten nails who asks for advice on how to stop this habit?
a. Most people are unable to stop.
b. Frequent manicures may motivate him or her to stop.
c. Placing bad-tasting powders on the nails can be effective.
d. This habit is hereditary.

20. The main effect of aging on the skin is
a. loss of elasticity.
b. increased amount of subcutaneous tissue.
c. increased blood flow.
d. loss of hair follicles.

21. Which of the following is an example of a seasonal condition?
a. acne
b. rosacea
c. herpes simplex
d. prickly heat

22. A callus that grows inward is referred to as a
a. cyst.
b. corn.
c. mole.
d. sarcoma.

23. The integumentary system includes the
a. skin and its accessory organs.
b. bones and muscles.
c. heart, lungs, and blood vessels.
d. digestive organs and glands.

24. As a cosmetologist, you need to understand the muscle structure of the face and neck in order to
a. avoid hurting your clients during chemical treatments.
b. choose the most attractive hair colors.
c. give an effective and relaxing massage.
d. apply makeup most effectively.

25. Which branch of the seventh cranial nerve affects the muscles at the base of the skull behind the ear?
a. temporal
b. infraorbital
c. posterior auricular
d. supratrochlear

26. The sweat and oil glands found in the skin are examples of
a. lymphatic ducts.
b. endocrine glands.
c. ductless glands.
d. exocrine glands.

27. A coloring technique that involves painting lightener on the hair with a tint brush or rattail comb is called
a. slicing.
b. weaving.
c. balayage.
d. foiling.

28. In hair coloring, when should you recommend a color filler?
a. before performing a tint back on lightened hair
b. before performing a retouch
c. before performing a reconditioning treatment on lightened hair
d. before applying a virgin tint when going darker

29. Which of the following hair-care substances has an acidic pH?
a. conditioner
b. semipermanent color
c. cold waving lotion
d. hair relaxer

30. Permanent waving works by
a. breaking and rearranging the hair's disulfide bonds.
b. stretching and reconfiguring the hair's H and S bonds.
c. coating the hair shaft with strong protein molecules.
d. completely severing the hair's disulfide bonds.

31. Which substance is capable of dissolving the greatest number of other substances?
a. water
b. oil
c. alcohol
d. glycerin

32. What should be used to presoften resistant hair to make it more receptive to hair color?
a. a dark shade of tint
b. 12% ammonia water
c. 20% peroxide
d. 20 volume peroxide

33. A complete business plan would include all of the following EXCEPT
a. a description of the proposed business.
b. a profit and loss statement.
c. the names and addresses of employees.
d. the number of employees and total salaries.

34. The largest expense involved in running a salon is for
a. insurance.
b. advertising.
c. salaries.
d. supplies.

35. The outer layer of the skin is called the
a. epidermis.
b. corium.
c. cutis.
d. true skin.

36. When you are using a hot wax for temporary hair removal on the eyebrows, the wax is applied and then removed with a fabric strip. In which direction is the fabric strip removed?
a. always upward
b. always downward
c. with the growth
d. in the opposite direction of the growth

37. To prepare a client for a haircut, what additional step is necessary after shampooing?
a. Remove the drape and brush both towels.
b. Remove the outer towel and replace it with a neck strip.
c. Fold and secure a third towel over the drape.
d. Remove the neck strip and replace it with a second towel.

38. Trichology deals with the scientific study of the
a. nails.
b. hair.
c. skin.
d. triangularis.

39. The technical term for bitten nails is
a. onychophagy.
b. onychauxsis.
c. pterygium.
d. onychatrophia.

40. How should a stylist approach selling additional products and services to clients?
a. knowing the additional commission he or she will make
b. with a smooth line about the benefits of the additional sale
c. with sincere concern for the client's needs
d. with disregard for whether or not the client needs the product or service

41. Start at the ________________ when manipulating the scalp during a shampoo.
a. nape of the neck
b. top of the head
c. sides of the head
d. front hairline

42. A shampoo with a pH higher than 7 is said to be
a. mild.
b. for dry hair.
c. acidic.
d. alkaline.

43. A cream rinse is occasionally used to
a. make the hair softer and easier to comb.
b. prevent shampoo buildup on the scalp.
c. correct the pH of the hair and scalp.
d. eliminate minor dandruff problems.

44. All disposable materials used during a manicure should be placed in
a. your pocket.
b. a central laundry receptacle for dirty linen.
c. a plastic bag attached to the manicure table.
d. the drawer of the manicure table.

45. It is important to use light pressure when working with a cuticle pusher or orangewood stick so that the
a. tools will not be bent or damaged.
b. nail bed will not be injured.
c. nail tip will not weaken and break.
d. nail polish will not be accidentally removed.

46. The purpose of nail wrapping is to
a. make the nails grow longer.
b. provide a base coat for nail polish.
c. provide an interesting texture to the nail.
d. protect the nail or mend a broken nail.

47. When applying press-on artificial nails, you should put the adhesive on the
a. underside of the client's nails.
b. inside of the artificial nails only.
c. center of the client's nails and inside of the artificial nails.
d. edges of the client's nails and inside of the artificial nails.

48. When giving a pedicure, you should loosen and push back the cuticles with
a. a metal pusher.
b. your fingers.
c. an orangewood stick.
d. a cotton swab.

49. Which massage movement is described as a deep, rubbing movement?
a. petrissage
b. friction
c. effleurage
d. percussion

50. Normal skin and a healthy scalp can obtain the greatest benefit from a massage once each
a. day.
b. week.
c. month.
d. year.

51. You should help your client to relax before a facial by
a. explaining your sanitary procedures in detail.
b. providing a pleasant, quiet atmosphere and speaking professionally.
c. providing printed literature on the benefits of facial treatments.
d. describing your training and experience in detail.

52. Which of the following is the correct procedure for a facial?
a. mask, steaming, massage, cleansing
b. cleansing, steaming, massage, mask
c. cleansing, massage, steaming, mask
d. cleansing, mask, steaming, massage

53. Your client has acne, and some of the pimples have come to a head and are open. You should
a. wear rubber gloves while working on the client.
b. refuse to give a facial while the condition is active.
c. use only nondisposable materials for the client.
d. give a facial only under a doctor's specific orders.

54. The correct procedure for applying gauze for a facial mask is to
- a. apply the gauze to the face, and then add the mask ingredients.
- b. mix the gauze with the mask ingredients before applying to the face.
- c. apply the ingredients to the face, and then cover with gauze.
- d. apply three layers of gauze to the face, add the mask ingredients, and cover with three more layers.

55. When a client prefers to wear a very dark or bright lip color, you should choose a cheek color that is
- a. brighter.
- b. darker.
- c. lighter.
- d. the same.

56. When you apply makeup on a client, your goal should be to
- a. promote the products your salon sells.
- b. make the client look like a favorite movie star.
- c. make the client look as if she has no bad features.
- d. minimize the bad features and maximize the good ones.

57. To correct a long, thin neck, you should apply a lighter shade of foundation
- a. on the face than on the neck.
- b. on the front of the face only.
- c. on the neck than on the face.
- d. on the sides of the neck only.

58. A discoloration that was previously called mold between the nail plate and enhancement is actually a bacterial infection called
- a. fringe.
- b. onychorrhexis.
- c. pseudomonas aeruginosa.
- d. onychosis.

59. A bacterial inflammation of the tissues surrounding the nail is called
- a. onychomadesis.
- b. onychoposis.
- c. onychia.
- d. paronychia.

60. Why does a blackhead appear black or dark?
- a. The oil in the blackhead has been there for a long time.
- b. The skin is not clean.
- c. The pores of the skin are too small.
- d. The pores of the skin are too large.

61. To be sure your client will be satisfied with a permanent, you should first
- a. show the client how you think he or she should look.
- b. tell the client how experienced you are at doing perms.
- c. discuss the client's expectations and lifestyle.
- d. be familiar with the latest, most fashionable hairstyles.

62. Concave rods will create a curl that is
- a. the same size throughout its length.
- b. tighter at the top than at the ends.
- c. tighter at the ends than at the top.
- d. extremely loose throughout its length.

63. Which of the following should NOT prepared for use during a client consultation?
a. styling books
b. hair swatches
c. mannequins
d. color mixing bowl

64. The length of time you should spend rinsing the lotion out of the hair depends on the
a. texture of the hair.
b. size of the rods.
c. manufacturer's instructions.
d. tightness of the curls desired.

65. Hair can be permed successfully if it has been
a. severely damaged.
b. treated with a sodium hydroxide hair relaxer.
c. treated with henna hair color.
d. tinted or bleached.

66. Very long hair can present a challenge for the colorist because the ends of the hair are
a. dark.
b. overporous.
c. coarse.
d. extremely dense.

67. Color shampoos may be used to add slight color to the hair, to brighten the color, or to
a. bleach away natural color.
b. permanently eliminate gray hair.
c. cover unwanted color tones.
d. preview the results of hair coloring.

68. Why is it necessary for a cosmetologist to be able to recognize the use of metallic or compound dyes on a client's hair?
a. The colors achieved cannot be duplicated at home.
b. These products conflict with professional hair-care products.
c. Hair treated with these products can only be lightened with concentrated hydrogen peroxide.
d. These products are illegal to buy or use.

69. You are using the cap technique for highlighting. To achieve a subtle effect, you would
a. apply very small pieces of foil.
b. use small amounts of toner.
c. lighten only the hair under the cap.
d. pull out only a few small strands.

70. A filler is used to correct the hair's porosity and to
a. cleanse the hair ends.
b. deposit a base color.
c. deep condition the hair shaft.
d. remove unwanted red tones.

71. Neutralization is a process that
a. speeds up a chemical reaction.
b. stops a chemical reaction.
c. removes heat from a chemical process.
d. adds acid to a chemical reaction.

72. The results of a positive skin test are indicated by
a. redness or burning.
b. a severe headache.
c. chest pain.
d. swollen feet and legs.

73. When you are formulating a color for gray hair, it is important to consider the
a. client's natural hair color before turning gray.
b. particular shade of gray in the client's hair.
c. length and condition of the client's hair.
d. price the client is willing to pay for hair coloring.

74. Which color neutralizes a too-orange color?
a. blue
b. violet
c. green
d. brown

75. Which type of hair-color product can lighten and deposit color in a single step?
a. semipermanent hair colors
b. natural henna products
c. hydrogen peroxide
d. oxidative hair color

76. A muscle controlled by will is a
a. voluntary muscle.
b. involuntary muscle.
c. cardiac muscle.
d. nonstraited muscle.

77. Your client has brown hair that is 20% gray. To achieve a natural-looking, all-over hair color, you should use a permanent color formulation that is
a. one level lighter than desired.
b. equal parts of the desired level and one level lighter.
c. the same as the desired level.
d. one level darker than desired.

78. Why would it be necessary to keep written records of a client's hair-relaxing treatments?
a. to ensure consistent and satisfactory future results
b. to protect the cosmetologist and salon from legal liability
c. to learn more about the chemical reaction involved
d. to learn how to increase the strength of the reaction

79. If rinse water gets into your client's eyes after a chemical hair-relaxing treatment, you should
a. rinse the eyes and refer the client to a doctor.
b. call for an ambulance immediately.
c. rinse the eyes with cold water.
d. call your supervisor immediately to examine the eyes.

80. What is henna?
a. a vegetable hair color
b. an aniline hair color
c. a progressive hair color
d. a metallic hair color

81. In haircutting, the first step in four-section parting is to part the hair
a. from ear to ear.
b. from the forehead to the nape.
c. across the crown.
d. vertically above each ear.

82. A client's hair is NOT to be thinned
a. at the top of the head.
b. if it is very curly.
c. if it has been tinted.
d. near the hairline.

83. What factor plays a major role in guiding you to the desired end result in haircutting?
a. the cutting guide
b. the head form
c. the hair texture
d. the scissor shape

84. Top and crown layering of long hair prevents the hair from
a. becoming frizzy in humid weather.
b. developing split ends.
c. becoming oily.
d. lying too close to the head.

85. Which of these is NOT a texture service?
a. permanent waving
b. finger waving
c. soft-curl permanents
d. chemical hair relaxing

86. A shadow wave is a
a. shallow wave with low ridges.
b. finger wave that is beneath another wave.
c. wave at the back of the head.
d. wave at the nape of the neck.

87. At what temperature does an acid wave process at?
a. heated temperature
b. room temperature
c. freezing temperature
d. below zero temperature

88. What type of perm creates a chemical reaction that heats up the perming solution and speeds up the processing?
a. acid balanced
b. endothermic
c. apple pectin
d. exothermic

89. How does the roller size affect the resulting curl?
a. The smaller the roller, the tighter the curl.
b. The larger the roller, the tighter the curl.
c. There is no relationship.
d. The relationship depends more on direction of roll than on size.

90. Which type of hairstyle should be recommended to a client with a prominent nose?
a. a swept-back hairstyle
b. an upswept hairstyle
c. a tight, pulled-back bun or French twist
d. a forward hairstyle with softness around the face

91. In designing a hairstyle for a client with very thin features, you should aim to
a. create an asymmetrical effect.
b. add width to the face and neck.
c. cover the face as much as possible.
d. add as much length as possible.

92. Before starting a thermal wave,
a. apply setting lotion.
b. back comb the section of hair to be waved.
c. comb the hair in the direction of the wave.
d. thoroughly wet the strand of hair.

93. Which portion of the hair is the hair shaft?
a. the hair that fits into the follicle
b. the hair that projects into the papilla
c. the hair that fits over the papilla
d. the hair that projects beyond the scalp

94. What is the epicranius?
a. a muscle
b. a bone
c. a nerve
d. a blood vessel

95. What would you use during blow-drying to give the crown hair a lift?
a. a round brush
b. a vent brush
c. a very large diameter brush
d. an air waver with comb attachment

96. To clean a pressing comb before and after each use, you should
a. use antiseptic.
b. place it in a sterilizer.
c. wash it with soap and hot water.
d. wipe it clean.

97. Pressing hair that is incompletely dried can result in
a. drying.
b. burning or smoking.
c. cracking or peeling.
d. splitting.

98. Where would you place the tape measure when measuring the circumference of the head to fit a wig?
a. at the forehead hairline and going all the way around the head just above the ears
b. at the nape of the neck and extending up to the forehead hairline
c. above the eyebrows and going all the way around the head
d. two inches above one ear and extending all the way around the head at that level

99. During hair braiding, what stage is the hair in when the end of the lock is totally closed and the hair is tightly meshed?
a. prelock stage
b. sprouting stage
c. growing stage
d. maturation stage

100. Which of the following is a knot or coil of synthetic hair, usually worn with another hairpiece?
a. chignon
b. braid
c. fall
d. bandeau

Answers

1. **d.** To work in a salon, cosmetologists must be free of contagious diseases, because those diseases can be transmitted by contact.
2. **b.** Good posture improves physical appearance as well as prevents fatigue and physical problems.
3. **b.** A closed, clean, dry container will keep implements sanitary until they are ready to be used.
4. **c.** Follow manufacturer's sanitation and disinfection of whirlpool foot spa and of thrones, as this bacterial infection is generally found to be harmless except in this type of environment.
5. **a.** Short, rod-shaped bacteria are known as bacilli.
6. **d.** Scabies is caused by a tiny mite that burrows beneath the skin.
7. **d.** HIV cannot be spread by ordinary social contact, such as shaking hands or kissing.
8. **b.** Always wash your hands between clients and after using the restroom.
9. **a.** You should not work on a client with an open sore unless a doctor certifies that it is not infectious.
10. **b.** Because bacteria can grow on bar soaps, liquid antiseptic soaps are the safest for hand washing.
11. **a.** HIV (Human Immunodeficiency Virus) enters the blood stream through cuts and sores and can be transmitted in the salon by unsanitary, sharp implements.
12. **c.** Sebaceous glands are the oil-producing glands in the skin and scalp.
13. **d.** A solution labeled as hospital-grade disinfectant with virucide and tuberculocide, EPA registered will ensure complete sanitation. Label may also include HIV-1 and hepatitis A, B, and C. This disinfectant has been EPA-tested against all organisms.
14. **b.** The hair's pigmented layer is the middle layer, or cortex.
15. **c.** Finger waving is the process of shaping and molding the hair into S patterns using only a comb, fingers, and waving lotion.
16. **c.** Hair is composed of the protein keratin, the same protein that is found in the nails and skin.
17. **c.** The average nail grows approximately $\frac{1}{8}$ = inch per month.
18. **d.** Temporary color does not contain analine derivatives; therefore, no patch test is required.
19. **b.** Frequent manicures are sometimes effective in helping people to stop biting their nails.
20. **a.** The loss of elasticity that occurs with age is the main cause of wrinkling and sagging.
21. **d.** A seasonal condition is triggered at particular seasons of the year; for example, prickly heat appears in hot weather.
22. **b.** A corn is a callus that grows inward and becomes painful.
23. **a.** The integumentary system is made up of the skin and the oil glands, sweat glands, hair, and nails.
24. **c.** An understanding of the muscles of the head, face, and neck will allow you to give an effective massage.
25. **c.** The posterior auricular nerve gives motor function to these muscles.
26. **d.** The exocrine, or duct glands, have canals for transporting the product of the gland to a particular part of the body.
27. **c.** Balayage, or free-form technique, uses a tint brush or rattail comb to paint lightener on the top layers of the hair. It is subtle and draws attention to the surface.
28. **a.** Color filler is recommended before a tint back on lightened hair to deposit the base color, usually a red color.

29. a. Most other hair-care substances are alkaline.

30. a. Permanent waving works by breaking and then rearranging the disulfide bonds (straightening breaks them without reconnecting them).

31. a. Because of its ability to dissolve so many other substances, water is referred to as the universal solvent.

32. d. To make resistant hair more receptive to hair color, presoften with 20 volume peroxide or presoftener mixed according to the manufacturer's instructions.

33. c. A business plan is a financial plan that you develop before you open a business.

34. c. Salaries are by far the largest expense involved in running a salon.

35. a. The epidermis is the outer protective layer of the skin. It is the thinnest layer of skin.

36. d. When waxing, remove the fabric strip in the opposite direction of hair growth and apply pressure with fingers to help with the pain.

37. b. Replace the outer towel with a neck strip before cutting the hair.

38. b. Trichology is the science that deals with hair, its diseases, and care.

39. a. Onychophagy is the technical term for bitten nails, an acquired nervous habit where the individual chews the nail or hardened cuticle.

40. c. A stylist should approach selling to clients with sincere concern for their needs and by recommending only what is truly in the client's best interest.

41. d. Begin at the front hairline and work your way down.

42. d. A pH higher than 7 is alkaline; the higher the pH, the harsher the shampoo.

43. a. Cream rinses and conditioners can make the hair softer and easier to comb.

44. c. There should always be a small plastic bag hanging from the side of the manicure table to hold waste materials.

45. b. Too much pressure on the cuticle can injure the nail bed.

46. d. Nail wrapping is done to protect a weak nail or mend a broken one.

47. d. Apply adhesive sparingly to the inside of the artificial nails and to the edges of the client's nails.

48. c. Use an orangewood stick to push back the cuticles gently.

49. b. Friction is a deep, rubbing movement.

50. b. Weekly massage provides the greatest benefit to the normal skin and scalp.

51. b. A pleasant, quiet atmosphere and a professional manner will help the client relax.

52. b. This answer choice gives the correct order of steps in giving a facial.

53. a. Wear rubber gloves and use disposable materials while working on a client with this kind of acne.

54. a. The correct procedure is given in this answer choice. Sometimes a second layer of gauze is placed above the mask ingredients.

55. c. When a client wears a very dark or bright lip color, choose a lighter coordinating cheek color.

56. d. Your goal is to make the client look his or her best.

57. c. Apply a lighter shade of foundation on the entire neck to create an illusion of fullness.

58. c. Pseudomonas aeruginosa used to be considered a mold, but it is actually a bacterial infection. It can be caused by implements not sanitized and contaminated with the bacteria.

59. d. Paronychia or felon is a bacterial inflammation of the tissues surrounding the nail. Pus is usually present. Dishwashers, bartenders, and healthcare workers who have their hands in water are prone to this infection.

60. a. The skin is the thinnest on the eyelids and thickest on the palms of the hands and soles of the feet.

61. c. Clients will be most satisfied if the final results meet their expectations and fit their lifestyle.

62. c. Concave rods will create a curl that is tighter at the ends.

63. d. It is not necessary to have a color mixing bowl during the client consultation.

64. c. The instructions will tell you exactly how long to rinse the lotion from the hair.

65. d. Hair that has been tinted or bleached can usually be permed successfully if you choose the right waving formula.

66. b. The ends of long hair may be overporous and may, therefore, accept color differently from the rest of the hair.

67. c. Color shampoos can cover unwanted tones, in addition to brightening the hair.

68. b. These products, which are used in the home but not in the salon, can cause adverse chemical reactions with most professional products.

69. d. To achieve a subtle effect, pull out and lighten only a few small strands.

70. b. A filler will correct the hair's porosity and deposit a base color.

71. b. To neutralize a reaction or a process means to stop it.

72. a. Redness, burning, itching, or blisters at the site are indications of a positive skin test.

73. a. The client's natural hair color will determine the undertones that are still present and that will affect how the hair receives the pigment.

74. a. Orange is best neutralized by blue, its complement on the color wheel.

75. d. Only oxidative hair color can lighten and apply color in a single step.

76. a. Voluntary muscles are muscles that are attached to the bone and are controlled by will.

77. a. Because the client's hair is still predominantly dark, it will be necessary to choose a color that is lighter than the desired level to achieve a natural-looking result.

78. a. The main purpose of record keeping is to ensure consistent results for the client.

79. a. If the rinse water or the relaxer gets into the client's eyes, rinse with water and refer the client to a doctor.

80. a. Vegetable hair color is classified as henna. It is obtained from leaves or bark of plants and is available only in black, chestnut, and auburn tones.

81. b. Part the hair first from the forehead to the nape of the neck.

82. d. If you thin the hair near the hairline, the thinning will show.

83. b. The head form or the shape of the head or skull, also referred to as the head shape, plays a major role in guiding you to the desired end result.

84. d. Top and crown layering of long hair prevents the hair from lying too flat on the head, making the look fuller.

85. b. Finger waving is a wet-setting technique, and no permanent texture change is initiated through a chemical reaction.

86. a. A shadow wave is a shallow wave with low ridges.

87. a. Acid waves process with heat.

88. d. Exothermic waves create an exothermic chemical reaction, with the addition of an activator that heats up the perming solution and speeds up the processing.

89. a. The smaller the roller, the tighter the resulting curl.

90. d. The client with a prominent nose needs softness around her face.

91. b. The aim should be to add as much width as possible.

92. c. Before making a thermal wave, comb the hair in the direction of the wave.

93. d. The hair shaft projects above the scalp.

94. a. The epicranius is the broad muscle that covers the top of the skull. It consists of the occipitalis and frontalis.

95. b. Use a vent brush to create a lift effect at the crown.

96. d. The heat of a pressing comb keeps it sterile as long as it is kept free of dirt and debris.

97. b. The hair can burn or smoke if it is pressed when wet.

98. a. The correct procedure is to begin at the front hair line, extend the tape measure to a point just above one ear, and continue down to the lower back of the head, above the other ear, and back to the starting point.

99. d. In the maturation stage, the lock is totally closed at the end and the hair is tightly meshed; after several years of maturation, the lock may start to weaken or come apart at the ends.

100. a. A chignon is a knot or coil of synthetic hair, usually worn with another hairpiece.

LESSON

8 COSMETOLOGY ADVANCEMENT FOUNDATION'S NATIONAL INDUSTRY SKILL STANDARDS

LESSON SUMMARY

In this chapter, you will find the Cosmetology Advancement Foundation's (CAF) National Industry Skill Standards for entry-level cosmetologists, along with some information about the foundation itself.

The following National Industry Skill Standards are printed with the permission of the Cosmetology Advancement Foundation. For the past several years, the CAF has been working hard to include these standards in textbooks and other educational cosmetology materials, with the goal of state boards universally accepting the standards and including them in curriculum, therefore promoting more uniform requirements for licensed cosmetologists around the United States.

The mission statement of the Cosmetology Advancement Foundation is:

"To support, develop, and take-on unified programs contributing to the image, growth, and development of the Professional Cosmetology Industry."

CAF continues to reach out to the community at large, promoting a positive image for cosmetologists and bringing greater awareness about the profession to schools and colleges around the country.

National Industry Skill Standards

Cosmetology Industry

Skill Standards and Illustrative Task Statements

Skill	Level of Standard	Illustrative Task Statement
Reading Comprehension *Understanding written sentences and paragraphs in work-related documents*	3	(1) Read and complete forms for employment, financial records, licenses, etc. (3) Read manufacturer directions, procedures, and precautions of selected products to perform a cosmetology service
Active Listening *Listening to what other people are saying and asking questions as appropriate*	6	(1) Communicate with vendors and manufacturers to obtain product information (2) Communicate with co workers to encourage a team atmosphere and team efforts (3) Schedule client appointments (4) Observe and listen to client to determine cosmetology needs (6) Utilize client feedback as a self-evaluation of performance
Writing *Communicating effectively with others in writing as indicated by the needs of the audience*	2	(1) Maintain a waiting list for client appointments (1) Maintain client records in written form (2) Fill out forms such as applications (2) Write professional letters to clients

Skill	Level of Standard	Illustrative Task Statement
Speaking *Talking to others to effectively convey information*	4	(1) Greet clients and give an overview of services and products available (2) Discuss maintenance and care of hair after services, including products, restrictions, and special care (4) Consult with clients to determine their cosmetology needs
Mathematics *Using mathematics to solve problems*	3	(1) Complete sales ticket for services and/or products (2) Maintain records of income, including tips, and expenses (2) Price products for resale (3) Determine most economical sale of products, using division and conversion units (3) Determine formula of solution for hair texture, porosity, and elasticity (3) Use geometry techniques to determine proper hair cut techniques
Critical Thinking *Using logic and analysis to identify the strengths and weaknesses of different approaches*	4	(1) Establish time requirements and prices for services (2) Maintain an appointment schedule (3) Evaluate clients and their requests to determine appropriate services and/or products (4) Determine reactions to solutions, procedures, or products by observing the client (4) Self-evaluation of performance and determining new approaches for improvement
Active Learning *Working with new material or information to grasp its implications*	4	(1) Subscribe to professional cosmetology journals and attend seminars to learn new hair designs and techniques (2) Learn about products through personal use (3) Use client feedback as a self-evaluation of performance (4) Consult with client to determine needs and expectations for services
Learning Strategies *Using multiple approaches when learning or teaching new things*	1	(1) Use a variety of teaching strategies to show clients how to care for hair, skin, and/or nails

Skill	Level of Standard	Illustrative Task Statement
Monitoring *Assessing how well one is doing when learning or doing something*	4	(1) Maintain and use a reminder system for daily schedules and tasks (2) Monitor various procedures to ensure positive results (3) Determine reactions to solutions, procedures, or products by observing client (4) Utilize client feedback as a self-evaluation of performance
Social Perceptiveness *Being aware of others' reactions and understanding why they react the way they do*	4	(2) Demonstrate respect for individual differences (3) Assist coworkers in resolving problems or conflicts (4) By observing clients, determine reactions to solutions, procedures, or products
Coordination *Adjusting actions in relation to others' actions*	3	(1) Maintain a work schedule and an appointment reminder system (2) Schedule client appointments (3) Adjust procedures to fit client needs and expectations
Persuasion *Persuading others to approach things differently*	2	(1) Suggest products and services or sell added services (2) Encourage client to change hairstyle, beauty regimen, or try a new service
Instructing *Teaching others how to do something*	1	(1) Teach client how to maintain hair, nail, or skin and proper product usage
Service Orientation *Actively looking for ways to help people*	5	(1) Greet clients and offer them refreshments (2) Accommodate waiting customers (3) Consult with clients to determine needs and expectations (4) Discuss available alternatives with the client when their expectations cannot be met (5) Provide services to meet the needs and expectations of clients
Problem Identification *Identifying the nature of problems*	4	(1) Review manufacturer procedures, directions, and precautions before performing service (2) Determine reactions to solutions, procedures, or products by observing client (3) Assist coworkers in resolving problems or conflicts (4) Identify signs of adverse health/safety conditions and take appropriate action or precautions (4) Analyze client needs for products and/or services

Skill	Level of Standard	Illustrative Task Statement
Information Gathering *Knowing how to find information and identifying essential information*	3	(1) Locate information sources for current cosmetology trends and information (2) Ask coworkers and other professionals for information and assistance (3) Consult manufacturer's directions and safety precautions for products
Information Organization *Finding ways to structure or classify multiple pieces of information*	2	(1) Organize work area based on sequence of services, use of equipment, or other logical approach (2) Organize client information to ensure efficient access to critical personal and health information (2) Utilize system for important information such as client records, income, tips, and expense records, etc.
Idea Generation *Generating a number of different approaches to problems*	3	(1) Describe different hairstyles to achieve a client's desired look (3) Incorporate various marketing strategies into a client development plan
Idea Evaluation *Evaluating the likely success of an idea in relation to the demands of the situation*	2	(1) Select products according to hair and scalp type and condition (2) Recommend services and products based on client's needs and expectations
Solution Appraisal *Observing and evaluating the outcomes of a problem solution to identify lessons learned or redirect efforts*	2	(1) Determine problems and outcomes by communicating with clients (2) Observe clients to determine reactions to solutions, procedures, or products (2) Give and receive feedback to increase cooperation
Operations Analysis *Analyzing needs and product requirements to create a design*	2	(1) Determine hair design through listening to client's requests (2) Recommend products and/or services to meet the client's needs and expectations (2) Use business records to evaluate business growth
Operation and Control *Controlling operations of equipment or systems*	2	(2) Use a variety of instruments and equipment to achieve various services
Equipment Maintenance *Performing routine maintenance and determining when and what kind of maintenance is needed*	1	(1) Change blades for razors (1) Sanitize instruments and equipment (1) Oil clippers/scissors
Visioning *Developing an image of how a system should work under ideal conditions*	3	(1) Understand how to conduct business using a salon team approach (2) Implement a time management plan based on normal working situations (3) Develop image of finished style needed to meet client's expectations

Skill	Level of Standard	Illustrative Task Statement
Identification of Key Causes *Identifying the things that must be changed to achieve a goal*	4	(1) Provide and encourage the use of a suggestion box (2) Contact past clients to determine customer satisfaction (3) Review processes and procedures while providing client services (4) Analyze records of performance and client retention to determine areas of improvement
Judgment and Decision Making *Weighing the relative costs and benefits of a potential action*	4	(1) Maintain professionalism while interacting with clients and coworkers (2) Identify precautions and safety measures needed to protect the client (2) Maintain an appointment schedule (3) Make decisions and plan actions based on the well-being of the entire salon or team (4) Develop a marketing, client development, or business plan
Time Management *Managing one's own time and/or time of others*	4	(1) Define time allotments for various services (2) Develop and maintain an appointment schedule (3) Adjust services or actions to accommodate adverse time conditions (3) Use available time to benefit salon operations or professional development when clients fail to show or cancel appointments (4) Evaluate appointment records and past performance to determine one's time efficiency
Management of Financial Resources *Determining how money will be spent to get the work done, and accounting for these expenditures*	3	(1) Determine potential income and expenses based on income structures (commission vs. salaries), service times, product usage, and other variables (2) Maintain financial records, such as daily cash report, weekly sales, monthly statements, and tax reports (3) Manage income to meet expenses and provisions for future endeavors successfully
Management of Material Resources *Obtaining and seeing to the appropriate use of equipment, facilities, and materials needed to do certain work*	2	(1) Properly use salon equipment, facilities, and products (2) Maintain product supply for client services, purchasing products in bulk quantities when appropriate (2) Inventory retail product supply and places orders accordingly
Hair Care *Performing routine care to enhance condition and appearance of hair*	3	(1) Shampoo and condition hair (2) Determine hair condition and type based on observation (3) Recommend or provide solutions to improper hair care regimens

Skill	Level of Standard	Illustrative Task Statement
Skin Care *Performing routine care to enhance condition and appearance of skin*	3	(1) Cleanse skin (1) Operate simple facial equipment (2) Determine skin condition and type based on observation (3) Apply basic skin treatment for the improvement of skin, including cleansing, toning, moisturizing, and massage
Nail Care *Performing routine care to enhance condition and appearance of nails*	3	(1) Give hand massage and cleanse nails (2) Manipulate the cuticle (3) Shape, condition, and polish nails
Hair Designing *Arrange hair to achieve artistic design*	4	(1) Blow-dry hair (2) Use wet and dry setting techniques to achieve final hair design; use thermal tools and products to achieve final hair design (3) Arrange hair through various styling techniques to achieve final hair design (4) Design hair dependent on the client's facial shape, individual style, and expectations
Hair Cutting *Shorten or shape hair using a variety of hair cutting techniques and equipment*	4	(1) Cut a one-length hair style (2) Cut hair utilizing angles and sectioning; create layered, graduated hair styles (4) Create length and shape dependent on hair texture, condition, growth pattern, and facial shape
Hair Removal *Removing hair using various techniques*	3	(1) Prep skin for hair removal and remove hair from the body; perform aftercare (2) Wax and tweeze hair to shape the eyebrow (3) Use depilatory products to remove hair from the body
Hair Additions *Adding hair using various techniques*	3	(1) Fit and style a hairpiece (2) Select an appropriate hairpiece based on client needs and characteristics (3) Use hair addition techniques to enhance hair volume
Chemical Reconstruction *Altering hair structure using chemical processes*	3	(2) Choose products and services for hair reconstruction dependent on the client's needs (3) Apply products and techniques to produce or remove wave and curl formation
Hair Coloring *Altering hair color using a variety of processes*	3	(1) Interpret color charts to determine appropriate formula needs (2) Analyze hair condition and recognize evidence of previous hair treatments (3) Apply color products to hair

Performance Guidelines

Five critical job functions were identified for the entry-level cosmetologist. Twenty performance guidelines were developed for these job functions. Each guideline includes performance indicators, the representative skill standards, knowledge, and abilities. Peformance indicators are observable task statements that are indicative of successful performance of the guideline and job function. The following are the performance guidelines divided by critical job function.

CLIENT SERVICE ***The entry-level cosmetologist provides a variety of services to meet the needs, well-being, and satisfaction of clients.***

The entry-level cosmetologist must consult with clients to determine their needs and preferences as they relate to cosmetology services.

Performance Indicators:

Greets client and gives an overview of services and products available
Observes and asks questions to determine the client's needs and expectations
Discusses the benefits and/or features of products and services
Uses visual media as appropriate to enhance communication
After establishing services to be performed and prices, asks for the client's permission to proceed

General Work Skills:	Industry Standard:
Active listening	6
Speaking	4
Social perceptiveness	4
Service orientation	5
Problem identification	4
Information gathering	3
Idea generation	4
Judgment and decision making	4
Industry-Specific Skills:	
Hair care	3
Nail care	3
Skin care	3

Generalized Work Activities:

Getting Information needed to do the job
Performing for or working directly with the public

Work Styles:

Achievement
Energy
Cooperation
Concern for others
Social orientation
Self-control
Independence
Analytical thinking

Knowledge:

Customer and personal service
Communication and media

Industry-Specific Knowledge:

Anatomy and Physiology

Abilities:

Oral comprehension
Oral expression
Originality
Problem sensitivity
Deductive reasoning
Auditory attention
Speech recognition
Speech clarity

The entry-level cosmetologist must conduct services in a safe environment and take measures to prevent the spread of infectious and contagious disease.

Performance Indicators:

Work area is clean and organized before each service
Safety and sanitary precautions are taken to protect clients and self
Personal protective measures, such as gloves, smock, etc., are used
Special steps to ensure client safety are taken when necessary
Client is draped and properly prepared for service
Equipment and instruments are sterilized and maintained prior to each use
Signs of infectious or contagious disease are identified and appropriate action or precautions are taken

General Work Skills:	Industry Standard:
Active listening	6
Social perceptiveness	4
Service orientation	5
Problem identification	4
Judgment and decision making	4

Generalized Work Activities:

Make decisions and solving problems
Organizing, planning, and prioritizing work
Assisting and caring for others
Performing for or working directly with the public

Knowledge:

Customer and personal service
Public safety and security

Work Styles:

Initiative
Concern for others
Dependability
Attention to detail
Integrity
Analytical thinking

Abilities:

Oral comprehension
Problem sensitivity
Deductive reasoning
Selective attention

CLIENT SERVICE ***The entry-level cosmetologist provides a variety of services to meet the needs, well-being, and satisfaction of clients.***

The entry-level cosmetologist must interact effectively with coworkers as part of a team.

Performance Indicators:

- Effectively works with coworkers to resolve conflicts
- Gives and receives feedback to enhance cooperation
- Shows respect for personal differences in others
- Takes initiative to facilitate cooperation and compromise within the group
- Involves and motivates coworkers in group efforts
- Participates in team activities, to advance team goals
- Makes decisions and plan actions based on the well-being of the entire salon or team

General Work Skills:	Industry Standard:
Active listening	6
Speaking	4
Social perceptiveness	4
Coordination	3
Service orientation	5
Problem identification	4
Information gathering	3
Solution appraisal	2
Judgment and decision making	4

Generalized Work Activities:

- Getting information needed to do the job
- Communicating with supervisors, peers, or subordinates
- Establishing and maintaining interpersonal relationships
- Resolving conflicts and negotiating with others

Work Styles:

- Cooperation
- Concern for others
- Social orientation
- Self-control
- Adaptability/flexibility
- Dependability
- Integrity
- Independence

Knowledge:

- Administration and management
- Customer and personal service
- Psychology

Abilities:

- Oral comprehension
- Written comprehension
- Oral expression
- Written expression
- Problem sensitivity
- Auditory attention
- Speech recognition
- Speech clarity

CLIENT SERVICE ***The entry-level cosmetologist provides a variety of services to meet the needs, well-being, and satisfaction of clients.***

The entry-level cosmetologist must effectively manage their time to provide efficient client service.

Performance Indicators:

- Develops and uses accurate time allotments when scheduling client services
- Demonstrates a respect for client's time by minimizing waiting time and performing services in appropriate time
- Maintains a waiting list to fill changes in schedule
- Maintains and uses a reminder system for daily schedules and tasks
- Uses available time to benefit salon operations or professional development when clients fail to show or cancel appointments

General Work Skills:	Industry Standard:
Active listening	6
Critical thinking	4
Monitoring	4
Social perceptiveness	4
Coordination	3
Service orientation	5
Judgment and decision making	4
Time management	4

Generalized Work Activities:

- Getting information needed to do the job
- Monitoring processes, materials, or surroundings
- Judging the qualities of objects, services, or persons
- Making decisions and solving problems
- Thinking creatively
- Developing objectives and strategies
- Organizing, planning, and prioritizing work
- Communicating with supervisors, peers, or subordinates
- Communicating with persons outside the organization

Work Styles:

- Persistence
- Initiative
- Energy
- Leadership orientation
- Cooperation
- Concern for others
- Social orientation
- Adaptability/flexibility
- Dependability
- Attention to detail
- Independence
- Analytical thinking

Knowledge:

- Administration and management
- Customer and personal service

Abilities:

- Oral comprehension
- Written comprehension
- Written expression
- Problem sensitivity
- Deductive reasoning
- Memorization
- Selective attention
- Time sharing

CLIENT SERVICE ***The entry-level cosmetologist provides a variety of services to meet the needs, well-being, and satisfaction of clients.***

The entry-level cosmetologist must take necessary steps to develop and retain clients.

Performance Indicators:

Develops a plan or strategy to retain clients and encourage the return of customers
Actively seeks client feedback and uses it as self-evaluation of performance
Develops a client record system and maintains current information on clients
Contacts past clients to determine customer satisfaction

General Work Skills:	Industry Standard:
Active listening	6
Writing	2
Critical thinking	4
Monitoring	4
Service orientation	5
Identification of key causes	4
Judgment and decision making	4

Generalized Work Activities:

Judging the qualities of objects, services, or persons
Analyzing data and information
Developing objectives and strategies
Documenting/recording information
Communication with persons outside the organization
Establishing and maintaining interpersonal relationships
Selling or influencing others
Performing for or working directly with the public

Work Styles:

Achievement/effort
Persistence
Initiative
Energy
Leadership
Orientation
Social orientation
Dependability
Independence

Knowledge:

Sales and marketing
Customer and personal service

Abilities:

Oral comprehension
Oral expression
Written expression
Problem sensitivity

BUSINESS OPERATIONS ***The entry-level cosmetologist participates in business operations including marketing, business development, and maintaining records.***

The entry-level cosmetologist must effectively market professional salon products.

Performance Indicators:

Identifies potential needs of clients and recommends appropriate products
Discusses products and their benefits with clients
Offers clients “best buy” suggestions based on cost per unit
Arranges products and merchandise to promote retail sales
Promotes the use of products through personal use
Maintains current information on products and manufacturers

General Work Skills:	Industry Standard:
Reading comprehension	3
Active listening	6
Speaking	4
Mathematics	3
Critical thinking	4
Active learning	4
Problem identification	4
Information gathering	3
Information organization	2
Operations analysis	2
Judgment and decision making	4
Management of material resources	2

Generalized Work Activities:

Judging the qualities of objects, services, or persons
Evaluating information for compliance to standards
Processing information
Making decisions and solving problems
Updating and using job-relevant knowledge
Handling and moving objects
Communicating with persons outside the organization
Performing administrative activities
Monitoring and controlling resources

Work Styles:

Achievement/effort
Persistence
Initiative
Adaptability/flexibility
Dependability
Attention to detail
Independence
Innovation
Analytical thinking

Knowledge:

Administration and management
Sales and marketing

Abilities:

Oral comprehension
Written comprehension
Oral expression
Written expression
Deductive reasoning
Inductive reasoning
Information ordering
Mathematical reasoning
Number facility

BUSINESS OPERATIONS ***The entry-level cosmetologist participates in business operations including marketing, business development, and maintaining records.***

The entry-level cosmetologist must maintain business records on client development, income, and expenses.

Performance Indicators:

Utilizes a system for maintaining records of income, tips, and expenses
Uses records to determine business growth
Accurately completes tax forms and reporting requirements
Maintains an organized system of important documents

General Work Skills:	Industry Standard:
Reading comprehension	3
Writing	2
Mathematics	3
Critical thinking	4
Monitoring	6
Information organization	2
Operations analysis	2
Judgment and decision making	4
Management of financial resources	3

General Work Activities:

Getting information needed to do the job
Evaluating information for compliance to standards
Processing information
Analyzing data or information
Making decisions and solving problems
Interacting with computers
Documenting/recording information
Performing administrative activities
Monitoring and controlling resources

Work Styles:

Achievement/effort
Initiative
Dependability
Attention to detail
Integrity
Independence
Analytical thinking

Knowledge:

Administration and management
Clerical
Economics and accounting

Abilities:

Written comprehension
Written expression
Problem sensitivity
Deductive reasoning
Information ordering
Number facility

PRODUCT KNOWLEDGE, USE, AND SAFETY ***The entry-level cosmetologist must demonstrate safe and effective use of a variety of cosmetology products.***

The entry-level cosmetologist must safely use a variety of salon products while providing client services.

Performance Indicators:

- Uses appropriate protective measures to protect self and client against product hazards
- Discusses benefits and features of products with clients
- Selects products according to the client's hair and scalp condition
- Conducts clean-up procedures including proper storage and disposal of products according to environmental and health safety guidelines

Generalized Work Activities:

- Getting information needed to do the job
- Identifying objects, actions, and events
- Monitoring processes, materials, or surroundings
- Inspecting equipment, structures, or materials
- Estimating the characteristics of materials, products, events, or information
- Judging the qualities of objects, services, or persons
- Evaluating information for compliance to standards
- Processing information
- Making decisions and solving problems
- Implementing ideas, programs, systems, or products
- Interpreting the meaning of information for others

General Work Skills:	Industry Standard:
Reading comprehension	3
Critical thinking	4
Active learning	4
Problem identification	4
Information gathering	3
Solution appraisal	3
Operations analysis	2
Testing	3
Judgment and decision making	4
Management of material resources	2
Industry-Specific Skills	
Hair care	3
Skin care	3
Nail care	3
Chemical hair reconstruction	3
Hair coloring	3
Hair removal	3

Work Styles:

- Cooperation
- Concern for others
- Social orientation
- Self-control
- Adaptability/flexibility
- Dependability
- Integrity
- Independence

Knowledge:

- Chemistry
- Biology
- Public safety and security

Industry-Specific Knowledge:

- Product knowledge
- Safety/health regulations

Abilities:

- Oral comprehension
- Written comprehension
- Oral expression
- Written expression
- Problem sensitivity
- Deductive reasoning
- Information ordering
- Memorization

PRODUCT KNOWLEDGE, USE, AND SAFETY ***The entry-level cosmetologist must demonstrate safe and effective use of a variety of cosmetology products.***

The entry-level cosmetologist must efficiently manage product supply for salon use and retail sales.

Performance Indicators:

- Maintains adequate product supply for client services
- Avoids product waste by using appropriate amount of product
- Purchases products in bulk quantities for salon use, when appropriate
- Routinely inventories retail product supply and places orders accordingly

General Work Skills:	Industry Standard:
Reading comprehension	3
Mathematics	3
Critical thinking	4
Monitoring	6
Problem identification	4
Information gathering	3
Information organization	2
Operations analysis	2
Judgment and decision making	4
Management of material resources	2

Generalized Work Activities:

- Judging the qualities of objects, services, or persons
- Evaluating information for compliance to standards
- Processing information
- Making decisions and solving problems
- Updating and using job-relevant knowledge
- Handling and moving objects
- Communicating with persons outside the organization
- Performing administrative activities
- Monitoring and controlling resources

Work Styles:

- Achievement/effort
- Persistence
- Initiative
- Adaptability/flexibility
- Dependability
- Attention to detail
- Independence
- Innovation
- Analytical thinking

Knowledge:

- Administration and management
- Sales and marketing

Industry-Specific Knowledge:

- Product knowledge

Abilities:

- Written comprehension
- Deductive reasoning
- Inductive reasoning
- Information ordering
- Mathematical reasoning
- Number facility

FASHION, ART, AND TECHNICAL DESIGN ***The entry-level cosmetologist produces fashion, art, and technical design by providing a variety of cosmetology services.***

The entry-level cosmetologist must provide basic skin care services.

Performance Indicators:

Cleanses skin using appropriate products and proper technique
Applies toners and moisturizers appropriate to skin type and condition
Uses proper technique in facial massage therapy
Discusses with client proper skin care

General Work Skills:	**Industry Standard:**
Critical thinking	4
Monitoring	6
Social perceptiveness	4
Service orientation	5
Judgment and decision making	4
Industry-Specific Skills:	
Skin care	3

Generalized Work Activities:

Monitoring process, materials, or surroundings
Performing general physical activities
Communicating with persons outside the organization
Establishing and maintaining interpersonal relationships
Assisting and caring for others
Performing for or working directly with the public
Providing consultation and advice to others

Work Styles:

Initiative
Energy
Leadership orientation
Cooperation
Concern for others
Social orientation
Attention to detail
Independence
Analytical thinking

Knowledge:

Customer and personal service
Chemistry

Industry-Specific Knowledge:

Product knowledge
Anatomy and physiology
Facials
Sterilization, sanitation, and bacteriology

Abilities:

Oral comprehension
Oral expression
Problem sensitivity
Finger dexterity

FASHION, ART, AND TECHNICAL DESIGN ***The entry-level cosmetologist produces fashion, art, and technical design by providing a variety of cosmetology services.***

The entry-level cosmetologist must provide basic manicure and pedicure.

Performance Indicators:

Sanitizes area, self, and client's hands
Sanitizes implements (instruments) before each use
Shapes, conditions, and polishes nails to the satisfaction of client
Massages and moisturizes hands, wrists, and arms
Discusses with client proper nail care

General Work Skills:	Industry Standard:
Active listening	6
Speaking	4
Monitoring	6
Social perceptiveness	4
Service orientation	5
Judgment and decision making	4
Industry-Specific Skills:	
Nail care	3

Generalized Work Activities:

Communicating with persons outside the organization
Establishing and maintaining interpersonal relationships
Assisting and caring for others
Performing for or working directly with the public

Work Styles:

Initiative
Energy
Leadership orientation
Cooperation
Concern for others
Social orientation
Attention to detail
Independence
Analytical thinking

Customer and personal service
Public safety and security

Industry-Specific Knowledge:

Product knowledge
Anatomy and physiology
Manicures
Sterilization, sanitation, and bacteriology

Abilities:

Problem sensitivity
Arm-hand steadiness
Finger dexterity
Near vision

FASHION, ART, AND TECHNICAL DESIGN ***The entry-level cosmetologist produces fashion, art, and technical design by providing a variety of cosmetology services.***

The entry-level cosmetologist must apply appropriate cosmetics to enhance a client's appearance.

Performance Indicators:

Sanitizes implements and prepares products before each service
Properly prepares skin before makeup application
Applies foundation and color according to client's individual skin condition, color palate, and style
Discusses with client proper makeup techniques

General Work Skills:	Industry Standard:
Speaking	4
Critical thinking	4
Monitoring	4
Social perceptiveness	4
Instructing	1
Service orientation	5
Visioning	3
Judgment and decision making	4
Industry-Specific Skills:	
Skin care	3

Generalized Work Activities:

Getting information needed to do the job
Monitoring processes, materials, or surroundings
Making decisions and solving problems
Thinking creatively
Communicating with persons outside the organizations
Establishing and maintaining interpersonal relationships
Performing for or working directly with the public

Work Styles:

Initiative
Energy
Leadership orientation
Cooperation
Concern for others
Social orientation
Adaptability/flexibility
Attention to detail
Independence
Innovation
Analytical thinking

Knowledge:

Customer and personal service
Design
Fine arts
Public safety and security

Industry-Specific Knowledge:

Product knowledge
Makeup design

Abilities:

Fluency of ideas
Originality
Problem sensitivity
Visualization
Arm-hand steadiness
Visual color discrimination

FASHION, ART, AND TECHNICAL DESIGN ***The entry-level cosmetologist produces fashion, art, and technical design by providing a variety of cosmetology services.***

The entry-level cosmetologist must provide a haircut in accordance with a client's needs or expectations.

Performance Indicators:

Conceives vision of finished style and appropriate steps to accomplish it
Selects and prepares equipment and products prior to beginning service
Applies a variety of cutting techniques to achieve the client's desired haircut
Accomplishes service in a standard amount of time
Maintains attention to detail throughout haircutting process

General Work Skills:	Industry Standard:
Coordination	3
Operation analysis	2
Equipment selection	3
Operation and control	2
Visioning	3
Judgment and decision making	4
Industry-Specific Skills:	
Hair care	3
Hair cutting	3

Generalized Work Activities:

Getting information needed to do the job
Thinking creatively
Updating and using job-relevant knowledge
Performing general physical activities
Handling and moving objects
Controlling machines and processes
Implementing ideas, programs, systems, or products
Interpreting the meaning of information for others

Work Styles:

Achievement/effort
Persistence
Initiative
Energy
Cooperation
Concern for others
Social orientation
Self-control
Stress tolerance
Adaptability/flexibility
Dependability
Attention to detail
Independence
Innovation
Analytical thinking

Knowledge:

Design
Mechanical
Fine arts

Industry-Specific Knowledge:

Anatomy and physiology
Hairstyling
Sterilization, sanitation, & bacteriology
Health/safety regulations

Abilities:

Problem sensitivity
Deductive reasoning
Selective attention

FASHION, ART, AND TECHNICAL DESIGN ***The entry-level cosmetologist produces fashion, art, and technical design by providing a variety of cosmetology services.***

The entry-level cosmetologist must provide styling and finishing techniques to complete a hairstyle to the satisfaction of the client.

Performance Indicators:

- Conceives vision of desired look and appropriate techniques needed to achieve it
- Uses a variety of finishing techniques to achieve the client's desired hairstyle
- Selects appropriate equipment and products prior to beginning service
- Instructs clients on procedures and/or products to ensure their satisfaction and ability to recreate the style
- Accomplishes service in a standard amount of time

General Work Skills:	Industry Standard:
Critical thinking	4
Coordination	3
Problem identification	4
Idea generation	4
Operations analysis	2
Equipment selection	3
Visioning	3
Judgment and decision making	4
Industry-Specific Skills:	
Hair care	3
Hair designing	3

Generalized Work Activities:

- Identifying objects, actions, and events
- Estimating the characteristics of materials, products, events, or information
- Making decisions and solving problems
- Thinking creatively
- Updating and using job-relevant knowledge
- Performing general physical activities
- Handling and moving objects
- Controlling machines and processes
- Implementing ideas, programs, systems, or products
- Interpreting the meaning of information for others

Work Styles:

- Achievement/effort
- Persistence
- Initiative
- Social orientation
- Self-control
- Adaptability/flexibility
- Dependability
- Attention to detail
- Independence
- Innovation
- Analytical thinking

Knowledge:

- Design
- Chemistry
- Fine arts

Industry-Specific Knowledge:

- Product knowledge
- Anatomy and physiology
- Hairstyling

Abilities:

- Originality
- Inductive reasoning
- Visualization
- Selective attention
- Manual dexterity
- Depth perception

FASHION, ART, AND TECHNICAL DESIGN ***The entry-level cosmetologist produces fashion, art, and technical design by providing a variety of cosmetology services.***

The entry-level cosmetologist must conduct a color service in accordance with a client's needs or expectations.

Performance Indicators:

- Proper protective measures for both self and client are used for every service—i.e., gloves, smock, etc.
- Equipment and products are selected and prepared before beginning service
- Correct formula of solution is chosen according to hair texture, porosity, and elasticity
- Manufacturer procedures, directions, and precautions are reviewed before performing service
- Client is observed to determine adverse reactions to solutions, procedures, or products
- Client is instructed on procedures and/or products to ensure their continued satisfaction
- Procedure is documented for client record, including colors and products used

General Work Skills:	Industry Standard:
Reading comprehension	3
Critical thinking	4
Coordination	3
Problem identification	4
Information gathering	3
Idea generation	4
Operations analysis	2
Equipment selection	3
Testing	3
Visioning	3
Judgment and decision making	4
Industry-Specific Skills:	
Hair care	3
Hair coloring	3

Generalized Work Activities:

- Getting information needed to do the job
- Identifying objects, actions, and events
- Monitoring processes, materials, or surroundings
- Estimating the characteristics of materials, products, events, or information
- Making decisions and solving problems
- Thinking creatively
- Updating and using job-relevant knowledge
- Performing general physical activities
- Handling and moving objects
- Controlling machines and processes
- Implementing ideas, programs, systems, or products
- Interpreting the meaning of information for others

Work Styles:

- Achievement/effort
- Persistence
- Initiative
- Social orientation
- Self-control
- Adaptability/flexibility
- Dependability
- Attention to detail
- Independence
- Innovation
- Analytical thinking

Knowledge:

- Design
- Chemistry
- Fine arts

Industry-Specific Knowledge:

- Product knowledge
- Anatomy and physiology
- Hair coloring

Abilities:

- Originality
- Problem sensitivity
- Inductive reasoning
- Visualization
- Selective attention
- Manual dexterity
- Finger dexterity
- Near vision
- Depth perception

FASHION, ART, AND TECHNICAL DESIGN ***The entry-level cosmetologist produces fashion, art, and technical design by providing a variety of cosmetology services.***

The entry-level cosmetologist must perform hair relaxation and wave formation techniques in accordance with the manufacturer directions.

Performance Indicator:

- Proper protective measures for both self and client are used for every service—i.e., gloves, smock, etc.
- Equipment and products are selected and prepared before beginning service
- Correct technique or formula of solution is chosen according to hair texture, porosity, and elasticity
- Manufacturer procedures, directions, and precautions are reviewed before performing service
- A test of formula is correctly made with client's hair
- Client is observed to determine adverse reactions to solutions, procedures, or products
- Client is instructed on procedures and/or products to ensure their continued satisfaction
- Procedure is documented for client record, including colors and products used

General Work Skills:	Industry Standard:
Reading comprehension	3
Critical thinking	4
Coordination	3
Problem identification	4
Information gathering	3
Idea generation	4
Operations analysis	2
Equipment selection	3
Testing	3
Visioning	3
Judgment and decision making	4
Industry-Specific Skills:	
Hair care	3
Chemical hair reconstruction	3
Hair designing	3

Generalized Work Activities:

- Getting information needed to do the job
- Identifying objects, actions, and events
- Monitoring processes, materials, or surroundings
- Estimating the characteristics of materials, products, events, or information
- Making decisions and solving problems
- Thinking creatively
- Updating and using job-relevant knowledge
- Performing general physical activities
- Handling and moving objects
- Controlling machines and processes
- Implementing ideas, programs, systems, or products
- Interpreting the meaning of information for others

Work Styles:

- Achievement/effort
- Persistence
- Initiative
- Social orientation
- Self-control
- Adaptability/flexibility
- Dependability
- Attention to detail
- Independence
- Innovation
- Analytical thinking

Knowledge:

- Design
- Chemistry
- Fine arts

Industry-Specific Knowledge:

- Anatomy and physiology
- Product knowledge
- Hair waving

Abilities:

- Originality
- Problem sensitivity
- Inductive reasoning
- Visualization
- Selective attention
- Manual dexterity
- Finger dexterity
- Near vision

FASHION, ART, AND TECHNICAL DESIGN ***The entry-level cosmetologist produces fashion, art, and technical design by providing a variety of cosmetology services.***

The entry-level cosmetologist must provide non-surgical hair additions.

Performance Indicators:

Selects appropriate hairpiece according to client's individual needs and style
Properly fits, styles, and adapts hairpiece to maintain a natural appearance
Instructs client on proper maintenance, application, and removal of hairpiece
Uses hair addition techniques to enhance hair volume

General Work Skills:	Industry Standard:
Critical thinking	4
Monitoring	6
Social perceptiveness	4
Coordination	3
Persuasion	2
Instructing	1
Service orientation	5
Solution appraisal	3
Visioning	3
Judgment and decision making	4
Industry-Specific Skills:	
Hair additions	3

Generalized Work Activities:

Monitoring processes, materials, or surroundings
Making decisions and solving problems
Thinking creatively
Communicating with persons outside the organization
Establishing and maintaining interpersonal relationships
Assisting and caring for others
Performing for or working directly with the public
Providing consultation and advice to others

Work Styles:

Initiative
Energy
Leadership orientation
Cooperation
Concern for others
Social orientation
Analytical thinking

Knowledge:

Customer and personal service

Industry-Specific Knowledge:

Hair replacement technology
Wiggery

Abilities:

Oral comprehension
Oral expression
Originality
Problem sensitivity
Visualization
Manual dexterity
Near vision

FASHION, ART, AND TECHNICAL DESIGN ***The entry-level cosmetologist produces fashion, art, and technical design by providing a variety of cosmetology services.***

The entry-level cosmetologist must perform hair removal services.

Performance Indicators:

- Selects, sanitizes, and prepares implements and products before beginning service
- Performs skin analysis and properly prepares skin
- Performs hair removal service to the satisfaction of client
- Performs after care, such as moisturizer, antibacterial lotion, etc., to promote the comfort and satisfaction of the client

General Work Skills:	**Industry Standard:**
Active listening	6
Speaking	4
Critical thinking	4
Monitoring	6
Social perceptiveness	4
Service orientation	5
Problem identification	4
Operations analysis	2
Judgment and decision making	4
Industry-Specific Skills:	
Skin care	3
Hair removal	3

Generalized Work Activities:

- Monitoring processes, materials, or surroundings
- Making decisions and solving problems
- Communicating with persons outside the organization
- Establishing and maintaining interpersonal relationships
- Assisting and caring for others
- Performing for or working directly with the public
- Providing consultation and advice to others

Work Styles:

- Initiative
- Energy
- Leadership orientation
- Cooperation
- Concern for others
- Social orientation
- Analytical thinking

Knowledge:

- Customer and personal service

Industry-Specific Knowledge:

- Anatomy and physiology
- Sterilization, sanitation, and electrology

Abilities:

- Oral comprehension
- Oral expression
- Originality
- Problem sensitivity
- Visualization
- Manual dexterity
- Near vision

PERSONAL DEVELOPMENT ***The entry-level cosmetologist must continue to develop personally and professionally to maintain a competitive edge in the cosmetology industry.***

The entry-level cosmetologist must participate in life-long learning to stay current of trends, technology, and techniques pertaining to the cosmetology industry.

Performance Indicators:

Routinely participates in industry related shows, fairs, seminars, etc.
Routinely participates in refresher courses for cosmetologists
Subscribes to cosmetology journals and professional organizations

General Work Skills:	Industry Standard:
Reading comprehension	3
Active listening	6
Critical thinking	4
Active learning	4
Social perceptiveness	3
Service orientation	5
Information gathering	3
Information organization	2
Idea generation	4
Idea evaluation	2
Visioning	3
Judgment and decision making	4

Generalized Work Activities:

Getting information needed to do the job
Making decisions and solving problems
Thinking creatively
Updating and using job-relevant knowledge

Work Styles:

Achievement/effort
Persistence
Initiative
Leadership orientation
Cooperation
Concern for others
Social orientation
Adaptability/flexibility
Attention to detail
Independence
Innovation

Knowledge:

Customer and personal service
Design

Industry-Specific Knowledge:

Personal development

Abilities:

Oral comprehension
Written comprehension
Fluency of ideas
Originality
Information ordering
Visualization

PERSONAL DEVELOPMENT ***The entry-level cosmetologist must continue to develop personally and professionally to maintain a competitive edge in the cosmetology industry.***

The entry-level cosmetologist must use appropriate methods to ensure personal health and well-being.

Performance Indicators:

Takes appropriate measures to protect personal healtl—i.e., use of proper work attire

Adjusts equipment and working area to meet individual requirements—i.e., adjusts chair to proper height

Uses equipment properly following appropriate ergonomics

General Work Skills:	Industry Standard:
Critical thinking	4
Monitoring	6
Coordination	3
Problem identification	4
Information gathering	3
Operations analysis	2
Operation and control	2
Judgment and decision making	4

Generalized Work Activities:

Getting information needed to do the job

Monitoring processes, materials, or surroundings

Making decisions and solving problems

Performing general physical activities

Performing for or working directly with the public

Work Styles:

Achievement/effort

Initiative

Energy

Leadership orientation

Self-control

Attention to detail

Independence

Analytical thinking

Knowledge:

Public safety and security

Industry-Specific Knowledge:

Product knowledge

Industry-specific equipment knowledge

Abilities:

Deductive reasoning

Manual dexterity

LESSON

COSMETOLOGY BOARDS BY STATE

LESSON SUMMARY

This chapter lists contact information of cosmetology boards for all states.

The following state-by-state table shows you contact information for your state's board of cosmetology. Please check your individual state to find out what licenses your state offers, what the required hours are, and the cost of becoming licensed. States change their requirements from time to time, so always confirm any information you find in this book with your state's board of cosmetology. See Lesson 1 for more information about the kind of written exams your state offers.

STATE	CONTACT INFORMATION
Alabama	Alabama Board of Cosmetology RSA Union Building 100 North Union Street #320 Montgomery, AL 36130 334-242-1918 fax: 334-242-1926 toll free: 1-800-815-7453 e-mail: cosmetology@aboc.state.al.us www.aboc.state.al.us
Alaska	Alaska Division of Occupational Licensing Board of Barbers & Hairdressers P.O. Box 110806 Juneau, AK 99811 907-465-2547 fax: 907-465-2974 e-mail: cindy_evans@commerce.ak.us www.commerce.state.ak.us/occ/pbah.htm
Arizona	Arizona State Board of Cosmetology 1645 West Jefferson Street Phoenix, AZ 85007 602-542-5301 fax: 480-784-4962 www.cosmetology.state.az.us
Arkansas	Arkansas State Board of Cosmetology 101 East Capital Avenue #108 Little Rock, AR 72201 501-682-2168 fax: 501-682-5640 e-mail: cosmomail.state.ar.us www.accessarkansas.org/cos/

STATE	CONTACT INFORMATION
Idaho	Idaho Department of Self-Governing Affairs Bureau of Occupational Licenses Owyhee Plaza 1109 Main Street, Suite 220 Boise, ID 83702 208-334-3233 fax: 208-334-3945 e-mail: kaksamit@ibol.state.id.us www.ibol.idaho.gov
Illinois	Illinois Department of Professional Regulations 320 West Washington Street, 3rd Floor Springfield, IL 62786 217-785-0800 fax: 217-782-7645 e-mail: tsanders@dpr084r1.state.il.us www.dpr.state.il.us
Indiana	Indiana Professional Licensing Agency Government Center South 100 North Senate Avenue Room 1021 Indianapolis, IN 46204 317-232-2980 fax: 317-233-5559 www.ai.org/pla/index.html
Iowa	Iowa Department of Public Health Cosmetology Board of Iowa Lucas State Office Building Des Moines, IA 50319-0075 515-281-4416 fax: 515-281-3121 e-mail: rbonanno@idph.state.ia.us www.idph.state.ia.us/licensure

STATE	CONTACT INFORMATION
Kansas	Kansas State Board of Cosmetology 603 Southwest Topeka Blvd, Suite 100 Topeka, KS 66603-3230 785-296-3155 fax: 785-296-3002 e-mail: kboc@kboc.state.ks.us www.accesskansas.org/kboc/
Kentucky	Kentucky State Board of Cosmetology 314 West Second Street Frankfort, KY 40601 502-564-4262 fax: 502-564-0481 e-mail: dena.moore@mail.state.ky.us
Louisiana	Louisiana Board of Cosmetology 11622 Sunbelt Court Baton Rouge, LA 70809 225-756-3404 fax: 225-756-3410 e-mail: lsbc@lsbc.state.la.us www.state.la.us
Maine	Maine State Board of Cosmetology Department of Professional Regulation (mailing address) 35 State House Station Augusta, ME 04333 (street address) 122 Northern Avenue Garniner, ME 04345 207-624-8632 fax: 207-624-8637 e-mail: linda.s.harris@maine.gov www.state.me.us/pfr/olr

STATE	CONTACT INFORMATION
Maryland	Maryland State Board of Cosmetologists 501 St. Paul Place, Room 202 Baltimore, MD 21202 410-230-6320 fax: 410-333-6314 e-mail: dllr@dllr.state.md.us www.dllr.state.md.us
Massa-chusetts	Massachusetts Board of Cosmetology 100 Cambridge Street, Room 1520 Boston, MA 02202 617-727-9940 fax: 617-727-2197 www.state.ma.us/reg/boards/HD
Michigan	Michigan Bureau of Commercial Services Board of Cosmetology P.O. Box 30018 Lansing, MI 48909-7518 517-241-9201 fax: 517-241-9280 e-mail: jecamp@michigan.gov www.michigan.gov/cosmetology
Minnesota	Board of Barber/Cosmetologist Examiners 133 East 7th Street St. Paul, MN 55101 612-297-7050 fax: 612-617-2607 www.state.mn.us
Mississippi	Mississippi State Board of Cosmetology 1804 North State Street P.O. Box 55689 Jackson, MS 39296-5689 601-987-6837 fax: 601-987-6840 e-mail: nluckett@msbc.state.ms.us www.msbc.state.ms.us

STATE	CONTACT INFORMATION
Missouri	Missouri State Board of Cosmetology 3605 Missouri Boulevard P.O. Box 1062 Jefferson City, MO 65102 573-751-1052 fax: 573-751-8167
Montana	Montana Board of Cosmetologists 111 North Jackson Street Helena, MT 59601-4168 406-841-2333 fax: 406-841-2323 e-mail: dlibsdcos@state.mt.us www.discoveringmontana.com
Nebraska	Nebraska Department of Health & Human Services 301 Centennial Mall South, 3rd Floor P.O. Box 94986 Lincoln, NE 68509-4986 402-471-2117 fax: 402-471-3577 e-mail: kris.chiles@hhss.state.ne.us www.hhs.state.ne.us
Nevada	Nevada Board of Cosmetology 1785 East Sahara Avenue #255 Las Vegas, NV 89104 702-486-6542 fax: 702-369-8064 e-mail: nvcosmbd@govmail.state.nv.us www.state.nv.us/cosmetology/
New Hampshire	New Hampshire Board of Cosmetology and Esthetics 2 Industrial Park Drive Concord, NH 03301 603-271-3608 fax: 603-271-8889 e-mail: lelliott@nhsa.state.nh.us www.state.nh.us/cosmet/

STATE	CONTACT INFORMATION
New Jersey	New Jersey Board of Cosmetology P.O. Box 45003 Newark, NJ 07101 973-504-6400 fax: 973-648-3536 www.state.nj.us/lps/ca/boards.htm
New Mexico	New Mexico State Board of Barbers and Cosmetologists Regulation and Licensing Department 2550 Cerrillos Road Santa Fe, NM 87505 505-476-4690 fax: 505-476-4645 e-mail: margie.sanchez@state.nm.us www.rld.state.nm.us/b&c
New York	New York Department of State Division of Licensing Services 84 Holland Avenue Albany, NY 12208-3490 518-484-4429 fax: 518-473-6648 e-mail: licensing@dos.state.ny.us www.dos.state.ny.us/
North Carolina	North Carolina Board of Cosmetology 1110 Navaho Drive Raleigh, NC 27609 919-850-2793 fax: 919-733-4127 e-mail: nccosmo@intrex.net www.cosmetology.state.nc.us

STATE	CONTACT INFORMATION
North Dakota	North Dakota Board of Cosmetology 1102 South Washington #200 P.O. Box 2177 Bismarck, ND 58502 701-224-9800 fax: 701-222-8756 e-mail: cosmo@gcentral.com
Ohio	Ohio State Board of Cosmetology 101 Southland Mall Columbus, OH 43215 614-466-3834 fax: 614-644-6880 e-mail: ohiocosbd@cos.state.oh.us www.cos.ohio.gov
Oklahoma	Oklahoma State Board of Cosmetology 2200 Classen Boulevard, Suite 1530 Oklahoma City, OK 73106 405-521-2441 e-mail: bmoore@oklaosf.state.ok.us www.state.ok.us/~cosmo/
Oregon	Oregon Health Licensing Agency 750 Front Street NE, Suite 200 Salem, OR 97310 503-378-8667 fax: 503-585-9114 e-mail: hlo.info@state.or.us www.hdlp.hr.state.or.us
Pennsylvania	Pennsylvania State Board of Cosmetology Professional & Occupational Affairs P.O. Box 2649 Harrisburg, PA 17105-2649 717-783-7130 fax: 717-705-5540 e-mail: st.cosmetology@state.pa.us www.dos.state.pa.us/

STATE	CONTACT INFORMATION
Puerto Rico	Puerto Rico Board of Examiners of Beauty Specialists P.O. Box 9023271 Old San Juan, PR 00902-3271 787-722-2122 fax: 787-722-4818
Rhode Island	Rhode Island Department of Health Professional Regulation Board of Hairdressing 3 Capital Hill Providence, RI 02908 401-277-2511 fax: 401-222-1272 e-mail: lindaa@doh.state.ri.us www.health.state.ri.us
South Carolina	South Carolina Board of Cosmetology 110 Centerville Drive, Suite 104 P.O. Box 11329 Columbia, SC 29211-1329 803-896-4830 fax: 803-896-4554 e-mail: jonese@mail.llr.state.sc.us www.llr.state.sc.us/
South Dakota	South Dakota Cosmetology Commission 500 East Capital Avenue Pierre, SD 57501 605-773-6193 fax: 605-773-7175 e-mail: cosmetology@state.sd.us www.state.sd.us/dol/boards/cosmo
Tennessee	Tennessee State Board of Cosmetology 500 James Robertson Parkway #130, First Floor Nashville, TN 37243-1147 615-741-2515 fax: 615-741-1310 e-mail: beverly.waller@mail.state.tn.us www.state.tn.us/commerce/cosmo/index.htm

STATE	CONTACT INFORMATION
Texas	Texas Cosmetology Commission P.O. Box 26700 Austin, TX 78755-0700 512-454-4674 fax: 512-454-0339 e-mail: diane.hill@txcc.state.tx.us www.txcc.state.tx.us
Utah	Utah Division of Occupational and Professional Licensing Department of Commerce 160 East 300 South P.O. Box 45802 Salt Lake City, UT 84111-6741 801-530-6628 fax: 801-530-6511 e-mail: dan.jones@utah.gov www.dopl.utah.gov
Vermont	Vermont Office of Secretary of State Secretary of State's Office of Professional Regulation 109 State Street Montpelier, VT 05609-1106 802-828-2373 fax: 802-828-2465 e-mail: ksanborn@sec.state.vt.us www.vtprofessionals.org
Virginia	Virginia Board of Barbers & Cosmetology 3600 West Broad Street Richmond, VA 23230 804-367-8509 fax: 804-367-6295 e-mail: barbercosmo@dpor.virginia.gov www.dpor.virginia.gov

STATE	CONTACT INFORMATION
Washington	Washington State Department of Licensing Division of Professional Licensing 405 Black Lake Boulevard P.O. Box 9026 Olympia, WA 98507-9026 206-586-6359 fax: 360-664-2550 e-mail: plssunit@dol.wa.gov www.dol.wa.gov/plss/cosfcont.htm
West Virginia	West Virginia Board of Barbers and Cosmetologists 1716 Pennsylvania Avenue #7 Charleston, WV 25302 304-558-2924 fax: 304-558-3450 e-mail: larryabsten@wvdhhr.org www.wvdhhr.org/bph.wvbc
Wisconsin	Wisconsin Department of Regulation and Licensing 1400 East Washington Avenue P.O. Box 8935 Madison, WI 53703-3935 608-266-5511 ext. 42 fax: 608-267-3816 e-mail: dorl@drl.state.wi.us www.drl.state.wi.us
Wyoming	Wyoming State Board of Cosmetology Hansen Building—East 2515 Warren Avenue, Suite 302 Cheyenne, WY 82002 307-777-3534 fax: 307-777-3681 e-mail: babern@state.wy.us www.state.wy.us

NOTES

NOTES

NOTES

NOTES

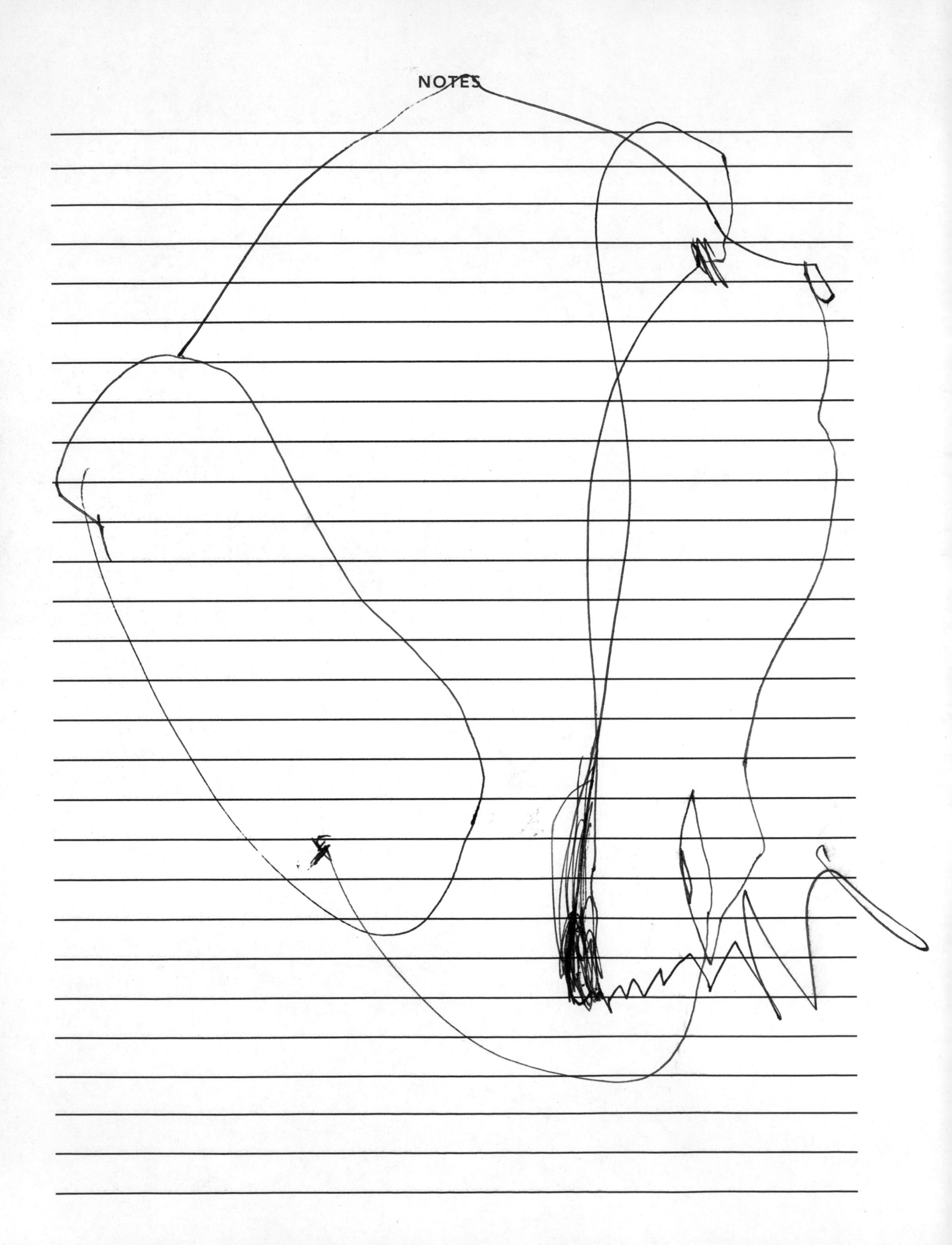
NOTES

NOTES

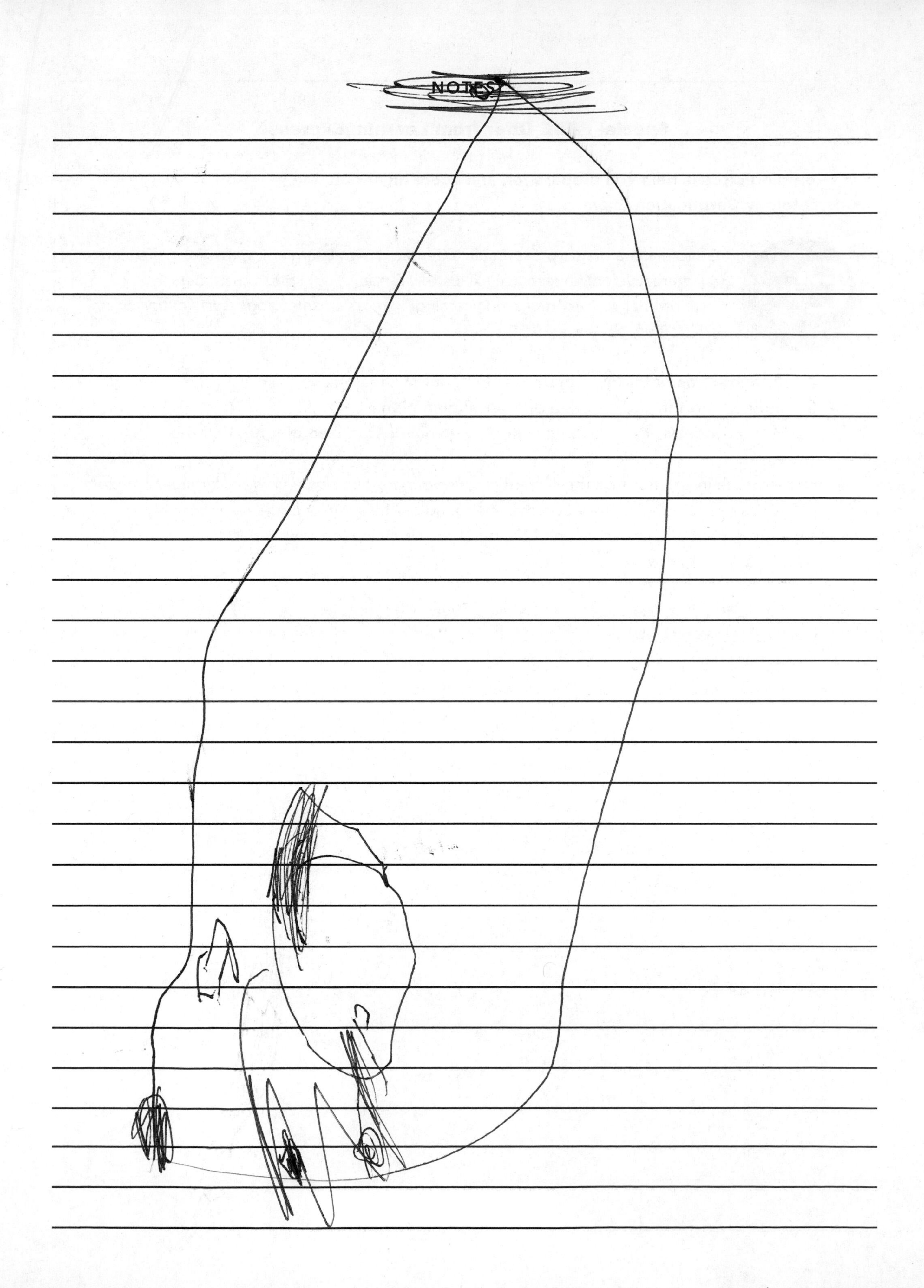

Special FREE Offer from LearningExpress!

Let LearningExpress help you prepare for, and score higher on, the Cosmetology Certification Exam

Go to the LearningExpress Practice Center at www.LearningExpressFreeOffer.com, an interactive online resource exclusively for LearningExpress customers.

Now that you've purchased LearningExpress's *Cosmetology Certification Exam, 4th Edition*, you have **FREE** access to:

- **A full-length cosmetology practice test** that mirrors the official Cosmetology Exam
- **Immediate scoring** and **detailed answer explanations**
- Benchmark your skills and focus your study with our **customized diagnostic report**

Follow the simple instructions on the scratch card in your copy of *Cosmetology Certification Exam, 4th Edition*. Use your individualized access code found on the scratch card and go to www.LearningExpressFreeOffer.com to sign in. Start practicing online for the Cosmetology Certification Exam right away!

Once you've logged on, use the spaces below to write in your access code and newly created password for easy reference:

Access Code: ________________ Password: ____________________

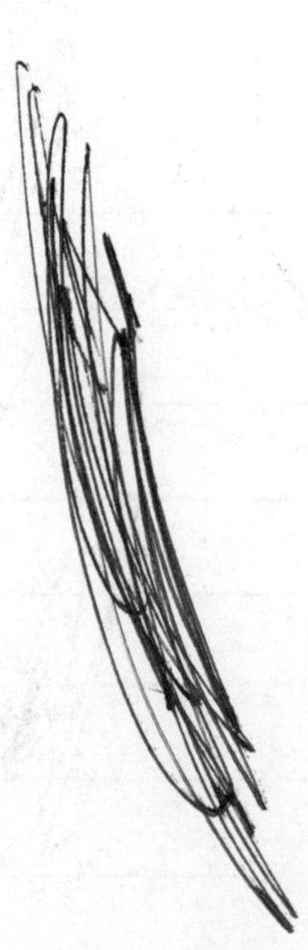